From the Other's Point of View

From the Other's Point of View

Perspectives from North and South of the Rio Grande

J. DANIEL HESS

Introduction by Eugene A. Nida
Photographs by Jorge Valenciano

Wipf & Stock
PUBLISHERS
Eugene, Oregon

Wipf and Stock Publishers
199 W 8th Ave, Suite 3
Eugene, OR 97401

From the Other's Point of View
Perspectives from the North and South of the Rio Grande
By Hess, J. Daniel
Copyright©1998 Herald Press
ISBN 978-1-5326-6661-2
Publication date 2/5/1999
Previously published by Herald Press, 1998

To

Victorio Araya Guillén
Juan Vianey Castro Carvajal
Zenón Chacón Badilla
Lilia Jiménez Arce
Flor Mendoza Mendoza
Doris Montero Segura
Humberto Pérez Pancorbo
Emilia Quesada Madrigal
Edwin Salas Brenes
Jorge Taylor Lemoent
Rodrigo Tomás Chacón
Jorge Valenciano Núñez

Contents

Introduction

From the Other's Point of View is important reading for anyone going south of the border to live or visit — in fact, it should be studied carefully by all who want to understand what communication is really about.

In seven chapters, based primarily on the richly documented accounts of real-life persons, Professor J. Daniel Hess covers the almost insuperable problems which separate and alienate North America from Latin America: poverty, economic imperialism, callous disregard for other values, and insensitivity to the suffering and the joys, the disillusionments and the hopes, the hatred and the love — all of which combine to make Latin Americans so difficult for North Americans to understand and appreciate.

But this volume is no mere collection of anecdotes — as fascinating as many of these are. A soundly scientific model of communication underlies both the analysis of problems of communication and the suggestions for solving many difficulties. The author includes well-documented evidence on the power plays of the United

Fruit Company in Central America; a highly personalized dialogue about liberation theology (with some startling statistics); the relation of grinding poverty to wetback immigration of a million persons a year from Mexico; and the selectivity and slanting of news from a Cuban World Festival of Youth.

This book on communication by a professor of communication really communicates—not only facts but feelings, not merely to the head but more so to the heart. Professor Hess does not claim to have all the answers—no one does—but his rich experience from living in Latin America and working extensively with Americans seeking to live and work south of the border has given him the insight required to alert us all to unsuspected aspects of our own cultural blindness.

What makes this book so important is that it shows not only how grossly we North Americans fail to understand Latins but also how much difficulty Latins have in trying to understand us.

The book also contains a section of shocking photographs with startling captions, but its realism comes from the series of impressive vignettes—brief episodes from real life, word-pictures which tell the story of Latin life more effectively than all the sociological statistics or the ponderous reports of government surveys could ever do.

Through reading this book you'll never again have your old point of view, but a more realistic and accurate perspective—and that is the whole point of *From the Other's Point of View.*

Eugene A. Nida
Translations Secretary
American Bible Society

Author's Preface

This book is about communication. Any person who wants to write about communication in the early 1980s — years that have followed an era of intensive communication research — must define some terms, because communication can have technical definitions, institutional definitions, psychological definitions, and on and on to the limits of the scholars' imaginations. And so for this book, we too shall define communication. Two persons in common union. Or, two peoples in common union. The first definition refers of course to interpersonal exchange; the second to intergroup exchange.

The study of communication, if you really want to be precise about it, isn't so much a study of communication but rather of noncommunication, or communication breakdown. Sometimes the textbooks refer to communication disorders. In such a manner, I may be writing more about noncommunication than of communication, for I begin my work with the observation that common union doesn't often occur across cultures, and that includes across the Rio Grande. Two people, born into two different families, nurtured in two different countries, conditioned by two different cultures, educated in two different political environments, supported by two different economic systems, baptized into two different religions—alas, what do these two persons have in common? The reader might think that easy travel, coupled with cheap tourist rates, would conveniently bring peoples of diverse backgrounds together. But easy travel and cheap tourist rates don't assure common union.

My intention in dealing with cross-cultural communication does not carry the presumption of my ultimately scribbling the prescription to end the malady. (If I could do such a thing, I'd have the State Department job of my choice.) Rather, I propose something of quite modest dimensions: to remind the reader that if we all knew a bit more about the nature of communication across cultures, we might not be so cavalier (arrogant, flippant, presumptuous) about our role in world community.

More specifically, I want to work with the concept of optics and optical illusion. All of us know the entertaining exercises in optical illusion. In the box shown to the right, do you see a box positioned as in A, or a box positioned as in B? Some people see one and some see the other. After concentration, you will probably see both. Here is another. Which line is longer, line A or line B? The accompanying lines confuse the eye. Both are equal in length.

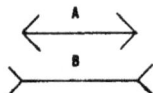

Version A   Version B

Such are the optical illusions of physics. I believe that there are cultural optical illusions as well. That is, one's cultural identity affects how one sees life. I shall give many examples throughout the book of simple phenomena that somehow register different "pictures" in the brains of people from different cultures.

It should become clear rather quickly that if two persons perceive things differently, they are likely talking to each other about two different things. No wonder communication breaks down.

The essays in the book do not try to destroy the various points of view. The great variety of perceptions really does add spice to international living. Rather, I hope to help people respond creatively by recognizing one's own vantage point for looking at life, by admitting that one's own vision isn't complete, by trying to glimpse the world from the other's point of view, and all the while by respecting one's cultural neighbor as one respects oneself.

In the second place, this book is about two specific cultures—the North American culture of the rural Midwest, and the Latin American culture as I have come to know it in Central America, largely in Costa Rica's central plateau. In a sense, the book is a case study of misunderstandings between *"Gringos"* and *"Ticos."* Eugene A. Nida, a widely respected linguist-anthropologist, has written:

> In comparison with the dramatic contrasts between the Orient and the Western World, between Negro Africa and industrialized Europe, and between the masses of India and the rural populations of North America, the differences between the Latin American and the North American ways of life seem minimal; and yet underlying these apparent

similarities are many significant contrasts, which from time
to time cause serious misunderstanding and tragic failures in
comprehension. Too often people in the Americas, rather
blindly assume that they are all alike."[1]

I have often returned to Nida's comment for comfort of
sorts when I have not understood what was going on
around me in Costa Rica, when I have felt like an outsider
and a foreigner (which has been most of the time), and
when I have assumed the superiority of my own cultural
habits and preferences.

As the culture of Latin America has revealed itself to
me, I have come to realize how indifferent (condescend-
ing?) we North Americans have been to the peoples of a
tremendously significant continental region. For example, our southern neighbors give us our daily breakfast:
coffee or hot chocolate, orange or pineapple juice,
margarine for the toast, bananas for the cereal. Yet that
southern neighbor who serves us is, to many of us,
nothing more than the breakfast servant. I hope this book
gives to the reader a more adequate picture of the human
grandeur in Latin America.

And third, *From the Other's Point of View* is about
peacemaking. The words "peace" and "peacemaking" do
not appear often in the text, nor do I offer explicit
strategies for peace. But I write with a painful awareness
of the bad communication between North and Latin
America, knowing all the while that much of the fault is
ours. When we North Americans have extended the hand
to Latin Americans in the twentieth century, too often it
has been a patronizing hand, a devious hand, a
pocket-picking hand, and even a violent hand. Our school
books camouflage from us the strange actions toward our
neighbors. It seems that every political initiative (such as

the Alliance for Progress), every well-intentioned economic initiative (such as the United Nation's Decades of Progress), and even religious initiatives (such as Protestant missions) have included good seeds mixed with thistle seeds, and the harvest has largely been disillusionment.

The Latin American response is confoundedly confusing—to our faces come smiles and bent knees; behind our backs there is submission, dependency, fear, and hatred. We and our neighbors remain religious, social, cultural, economic, and political strangers—and at times, enemies. Blessed are the peacemakers, for they shall inherit even North and South America.

A final word. I shall dare to hope for a response to this book similar to the response made to a "sermon" I once preached in San Jose. About to leave the country after 22 months, I was asked to give my farewell. For the occasion, I analyzed Costa Rica's "state of the union," pinpointing as precisely as I could the agenda for the country, including both temporal and spiritual dimensions. I tried to be creatively critical. Later I learned that at a women's meeting that same afternoon, a parishioner who was native to Costa Rica, said, "It was plain to me that he respects our country." I hope the reader of this book, as a result of my own respect for Latin America, will grow in appreciation for other cultures and peoples, and try the harder to be a person in union with those who have a different point of view.

Foreword

From Philippians 2

If then our common life in Christ yields anything to stir
the heart,
    any loving consolation,
    any sharing of the Spirit,
    any warmth of affection or compassion,
fill up my cup of happiness
    by thinking and feeling alike,
    with the same love for one another,
    the same turn of mind,
    and a common care for unity.
There must be no room for rivalry and personal vanity
among you, but you must humbly reckon others better
than yourselves.

Look to each other's interest and not merely to your own.

A song based on Philippians 2

Jesus help us live in peace.
From our blindness set us free.
Fill us with your healing love.
Help us live in unity.

Many times we disagree.
O'er what's right or wrong to do.
It's so hard to really see
From the other's point of view.

How we long for pow'r and fame,
Seeking ev'ry earthly thing
We forget the One who came
As a servant, not a King.

Jesus help us live in peace.
From our blindness set us free.
Fill us with Your healing love.
Help us live in unity.

by Gerald Derstine

Impressions

*Anecdotes in cross-cultural confusion,
as seen from the North American's and
the Latin American's point of view*

I have spent four of the past ten years working with North American students in a Latin American setting— Costa Rica. In that role I have formed memorable friendships with many people from north and south of the Rio Grande. Thanks to the students whose curiosity coupled with energy and resilience helped them "get into" Latin American culture, I have become acquainted with many Costa Ricans to a degree that would have been impossible had I and my family lived in Latin America "unattached."

A valuable part of these friendships has been the sharing of cultural shocks, the committing of cultural errors, the enjoying of another way of life, the resolving of cultural misunderstandings. These experiences have added up to a tale to be told.

In this chapter, I'd like to relate some of the tales. Let's call them exposures that capture a picture of life. I have discovered that if one sends the "film" to the lab for careful development, one finds some surprises. The pictures may reveal more than one point of view. In other words, some ordinary incident — something as ordinary as the wearing of a tie-dye T-shirt — may seem to the North American student as nothing more than the wearing of a tie-dye T-shirt. To the Latin American *señora*, it also is the wearing of a tie-dye T-shirt, but what she sees is something altogether different from what the student sees. Strange, isn't it. Particularly when one realizes that both people have 20-20 physical vision.

So it is that many ordinary incidents can be perceived quite differently. At the point in my own experience when I first realized this ever-present confusion, I was tempted to retreat. But retreat leads to paralysis. Later I began looking for these optical illusions and double exposures and divergent perspectives in culture, and then my own enjoyment of a foreign world was greatly enhanced.

As we move through the picture album, I will not stop to deal with the scholarly concepts of *frames of reference, psychological constructs,* and the theories of *group homogeneity and conformity.* Chapter Two will cover some of these.

Keep in mind that nothing is fiction in the accounts that follow. It all happened, and happens. I have, however, changed certain facts, compiled several incidents into one incident, altered the names of people, and in some instances added information so that the reader may understand a context.

We'll begin with cases involving students and their hosts. How entertaining it would be for you to peek from behind a curtain on the first day that students arrive in Latin America, and watch the greetings between student

and host family. The bashful, reserved North American.
The laughing, hugging, kissing, chattering Latin American. And neither of the two can quite bring the act off
without a participating partner! We'll begin with the first
case, one involving *friendliness.*

Case 1

Señora Monica de Rodriguez (host mother):
We like Suzanne much better than we liked Rachel in our
home. Rachel was a person very serious and studious and
cultured and of course very intelligent. She would read by
the hour. We'd say, "Come Rachel, let's do this" or "Let's do
that," but she wanted to read alone in her room. Suzanne?
What a friendly person. She calls us mami and papi, she says
good morning and good-bye and good night and always asks
how we are. She wants to know how we prepared the food,
and who is in the picture on the wall, and what the
announcer said on TV and why the joke is funny. On Sunday
at grandma's—we go there every Sunday, you know—she
told all the others how much she liked living here.

Rachel:
I enjoyed my stay in the Rodriguez home . . . except for
doña Monica's constant nagging: "Do you like this?" "Do you
like Costa Rica?" "Are you happy here?" I told them
everything was okay. Why couldn't they believe me? I'm not
a chatterbox, I'm not one to exaggerate. I try to communicate
with a smile or something. But I'm not a fussy *Latina.* Why
can't they let me be the way I am?

Friendliness to the North American rural midwes-
terner may consist of a quiet warmth. But to the Latin
American, friendliness doesn't occur until it is expressed.
As one student wrote in her journal, "The Latin American
stereotype of North Americans is that we are cold,
unfeeling, unexpressive. Here, the *word* is needed."

Frequently, the expression goes beyond words to include touch, a kiss, or a gift.

Case 2 deals with *dirt*. One of the North American's first impressions is, "Yuck, this place is dirty."

Case 2

Bob:

Latin Americans are dirty. There's garbage on the streets, litter on restaurant floors, paper and banana peels all over the park. Like a stadium after a baseball game. No garbage cans. People just pitch the junk. I read a sign in the bus, "Show your refinement: don't throw your garbage on the floor, throw it out the window." There's dirt at home too, and I'm surprised about that. I can't find wastebaskets. The kitchen—it's the crudest room in the house. The maid "washes" dishes by running cold water over them. And the people—I guess it's the grease on their hair that makes them seem dirty.

Señora Magda de Elizondo (host mother):

No, I can't criticize the North American students who've been in our home. They are a wonderful people, good models for our own boys . . . except in one thing. I hope you will pardon my bluntness. They do not pay attention to personal hygiene. They don't shower every day. Roberto, for example, goes three or four days without a shower. And what can I say about their dirty, torn, faded clothing? And their underwear. It should be washed daily. Shoes? I can't understand why a smart lad such as Roberto would not shine his shoes. Of course he sometimes wears tennis shoes, and when he does I prefer not to be seen with him. And he puts his shoes on the chairs and even on the coffee table.

Who would have thought that there is more than one way of looking at dirt! Latin Americans scrub and scrub and wax and wax their tile floors, wondering all the while how we can bear to live on carpets laden with years of dirt.

High-consumer North Americans, who are as dependent upon garbage cans as they are upon Kleenex, look in vain for places in Latin America to discard their trash.

Earlier in this book, I referred to tie-dye T-shirts, and doña Magda complained about clothing. Here is a case study on *clothing*.

Case 3

Sr. Manuel Antonio Mora (host brother, now a lawyer):

If you have dealings with North Americans, you will have to be prepared for their strange ways of dressing. They walk barefooted around the house, and sometimes in their undershirt. They will go to mass or even to a fiesta in jeans and tennis shoes. Last year I invited a North American friend to go with me to the national theater to hear a string quartet. The theater is our national gem, so we respect it very much. Well, in honor of my friend and of this occasion, I rented a tux and bought 75-colon balcony tickets. Can you imagine my face when Eric arrived in jeans and tennis shoes, and a shirt hanging out of his pants?

Eric:

I've been trying my best to be on the same level as my Latin American friends. I take an interest in their activities, and make as many friends as possible. And I'll admit, I've often lied about my family's wealth in the United States, just so they wouldn't feel inferior here. After all, we are equals. For example, I try to wear simple casual clothing. That way there isn't this big distance-thing.

The next case is about *foods and eating*—surely one of the most confusing aspects of living with a Latin American family.

Case 4

Alice:

At my home in the United States and on the college

campus I love mealtime—a tasty salad, good conversation, relaxation. But in my house here, I dread mealtime. The family doesn't eat together. Whenever someone is hungry, the *señora* or the maid fixes something. If more than one person is at the table, each one reaches for food but doesn't pass it. Very little conversation takes place. Often the *señora* is there watching over every bite I take. The food? Potatoes, rice, macaroni, and bread pudding at the same meal, with no fruit or salad. I've gained 10 pounds in a month.

Señora Yamileth de Abarca
   She doesn't eat! I have never seen a person like her. A bite of this, a nibble at that. The poor girl is going to get sick. She's so thin. I try to coax her, but I don't think she likes the food. I will always be ashamed to think that a guest of ours left here undernourished.

We could continue with case study after case study obtained from the living arrangements of students. The reader may wish to consult the excellent studies made by Raymond L. Gorden in Columbia (*Living in Latin America)*[1] in which he analyses "scenes" of guest-host miscommunication in the use of household space, such as the bathroom, the bedroom, the living room, and the dining room.

Let's shift our attention to several *roles* found in the typical household—the role that a person is expected to play, not because of his or her personality, but because of position in the household. That is, there are unacceptable and acceptable roles for the child, for the mother, for the father, for the maid, and, as students sometimes learn the hard way, for the guest.

Case 5

John:
   I felt rather bad about my visit to don Rodolfo's house. You see, he had invited me a couple of times to go see his *finca*, so

when he met me on the street on Saturday morning, he said *vamanos* and off we went. It was interesting—his *plátanos,* and *frijoles,* the pigs he's trying to fatten without corn. We were gone all morning, and in fact didn't get back into town till 2 or 3 in the afternoon. I thought that was it, but no, he wanted to give me lunch. Okay, we could go to a town restaurant for rice and beans (I had some *colones* with me) but no again, we'd eat at his house. We got there just as his wife was returning from the capital. She had gone to the doctor, I think, and had traveled on that frightful bus four hours. She looked beat. And then I couldn't believe what happened. He told her to make a meal. I started to protest, but he'd hear nothing of it. Sometime later there was a table full of food, yet Rodolfo hadn't lifted a finger except to offer me a drink.

Sr. Rodolfo Chacon:
   North American men have spoiled their women, and now they will suffer. The women will become their rulers. It's pathetic to see a man washing dishes. When a man comes home from work, he deserves to be attended. Imagine, having to do the laundry or even change a diaper. Those men will become effeminate.

How can an outsider quickly readjust his own focus to see things in the same way as the local people? That's a good question for which I wish I had a good answer. Until that answer is provided, I can only try to help students by giving them "homework" that requires them to stop-look-listen. Here are typical questions: Who commands whom? Who touches whom? When is laughter accepted? When is it okay to be loud? Whom should you not talk to? Not touch? Not laugh with? It is the intention, of course, to make students more observant of little things that they would otherwise miss. Once they begin looking, they see even more than they looked for, as Wendy illustrates nicely in her analysis of children in the home.

Case 6

Wendy:

My first reaction to the children in my home was that they were miserably spoiled, victims of overindulgent parents whose threats soon turned to sweetness. The kids had the run of the place. But then when I met children of other families, I noticed the same energy, the same indulgences. Was it a cultural thing? It seemed strange to me to let children run and scream and fight and climb and beg . . . and always win. I held this tentative explanation in the back of my mind, hoping for more data. Then I visited the public school. Wow! It was a chicken house of noise. You could hear it a block away. Everybody was talking at once. The teacher was no more vexed than the parents. In fact, there seems to be an encouragement of an uninhibited lifestyle. At first I didn't like this notion, but I saw the other side of the picture on Sunday at children's theater. The children participated so freely, calling up to the actors, and the actors responding to them. The actors depended upon the spectators to help solve a mystery actually in the play! I just can't imagine that happening to bashful kids in the States.

Wendy is making a lot of progress in perceiving the Latin American world from another point of view. There is, however, one particular family role that few, if any, students, have come to understand—the role of the maid. Here is a case study.

Case 7

Sr. Enrique Zamora:

Our maid left us. I think it's funny, although the *señora* is quite upset that there is no one to do the work. It's hard to find a good maid. This girl was a good one; she had been with us for about five months. Then a North American student became a guest in our home, and out of ignorance I suppose, he started talking to her as though she were a member of the family. He actually went into the kitchen to talk with her. I should have said something, but didn't know what to say. One afternoon they took a walk around the block! I told him then that it wasn't proper, but his Spanish wasn't good enough to understand what I was meaning. Then I took him with me to a party where 'he had a good time, and the next day he told the *señora* about it, and she teased him about the *señoritas*. The maid heard it all, and was terribly upset because she thought he was going to marry her and take her along back to the United States. She did not come back the next morning.

Paul:

Needless to say, I am stunned about Flora's quitting. If I knew where she lived, I'd go talk with her. She totally misunderstood my intentions. I wanted to be a friend, for I realized that she was being treated as a slave. She worked from six to six, yet they never treated her kindly. She didn't eat with us, never sat in the living room, never watched television, and I seldom heard conversations even between the *señora* and her. I felt sorry for her, but now I really botched things up for her. But maybe it will turn out okay if she gets a better job.

Family roles in Latin America are sometimes prescribed by social stratification, in which each person is given a level in which to operate. In the United States and Canada, the variety of roles and responsibilities defy easy categories. For this reason, the North American student can be jolted by the position he or she is given in the Latin American family.

Case 8

Rebecca:

I am so uncomfortable in my home that I'd like you to transfer me. The family is wonderful, no problems there. And I love the neighborhood. But I know that they can't afford to have a guest. I'm not sure what the *señor's* job is, but I know he doesn't earn much. The house is wooden, and in the back the walls don't go the whole way up to the roof. Birds often come in. Two girls—aged 10 and 12—sleep together in a cot so that I can have their bed. My "room" is partitioned off by dressers on one side and kitchen cabinet on the other. There's an outside toilet. In the morning, the children must wait for their shower till I take mine, so that I'm sure to have water (it always runs out before they all finish). They feed me special foods which the others don't get. It's awful. I'll get a piece of meat, and the children get rice and beans. They look at my plate and watch me. I intentionally leave food in the serving dish, and when I get up from the table, they clean up what is left over. Now they tell me they want to take me to the coast. It's improper for them to impoverish themselves for me. I'm rich compared with them.

Sr. Federico Acuña:
   You can't know how you honored us by asking us to receive Rebecca. What a pleasure to receive her not as a guest, but as a daughter. All that we have is hers. To see her enjoying life here gives us a satisfaction that nothing else could supply. When she leaves, she will carry part of us with her.

   Can you imagine the cruel disillusionment in the Acuña family when Rebecca finally returns to the United States, but doesn't bother to send a thank-you letter to them? That has occurred time and again in our experience, for the students have thought that a verbal thank you at the airport was sufficient.
   Case 8 guides us into another area for case studies—*the meaning of and response to hospitality.* To preface this section, it is well for us to recognize that the forms of hospitality in the United States have changed drastically in recent decades. I have many memories of Sunday dinner invitations, of extended stays by relatives. "Company's coming" was exciting news. But we have moved away from a company orientation to a more superficial party orientation that is less consequential and less involving. It is understandable that students should

not fully understand the character of more traditional hospitality. What happens, then, when the North American is guest of the Latin American?

Case 9

Jenny:

Some things here really space me out. For instance, this is a land of bananas, fresh oranges, the sweetest pineapples on earth, papaya, mangos—you name the tropical fruit and it's here. Well, last night my friend Cassandra wanted me to meet her special uncle and aunt. She talks about them all the time. We walked over to their *barrio,* and no sooner did we sit down than her aunt motioned her son and sent him out. I knew it was for food. In a thousand guesses, you couldn't name what we had. She served us, with the look of the greatest pleasure, little bowls of canned Libby's fruit cocktail!

Cassandra:

Jenny is a fine friend, but she is discourteous at times. Those times come at the worst of moments. Last night Tia Mimi wanted to do something *muy simpática* for my friend, so she paid a day's grocery bill to buy a can of imported fruit—pears and apples and cherries and peaches. When she served it, Jenny shrugged her shoulders. I thought she was going to reject the gift. How can I explain to Tia that Jenny really is a nice girl?

The issue of confusion in Case 9 was the "meaning" of a can of fruit. Many times gifts have passed from host to student, and most of those times, host and student put different values upon the gifts.

Hospitality—both at the giving and the receiving end—involves a certain amount of *time,* and as Edward Hall in *The Silent Language*[2] has pointed out, each culture has its own clocks. Case 10 has to do with hospitality wrecked by a clock.

Case 10

Señora Emilia Gutierrez:

What went wrong today? Did we offend them? Wasn't the hospitality correct? Are they accustomed to something better? Did the food make one of them ill, and they were afraid to tell me? Was it our dogs who frightened their baby? I don't know. They left so suddenly in the early afternoon.

The author:

I admit, I can't tell Latin American time. Mrs. Gutierrez told us to come Sunday. We asked what time and she said "early before the rains so we can take a drive." We thought 10 would be about right, but to be safe, we went at 10:30. Obviously we caught them unprepared. Nobody was ready for us. We sat around till I assumed they had forgotten about the drive. Wrong again. At 11:30 Señor Gutierrez jumped up announcing the drive. There was fussing and arguing who'd go, who'd stay home, which vehicles, which roads. The *señora* said she'd stay home to have dinner ready at noon, which I was glad about because I was already hungry, and sometimes those drives never end.

We finally took off in two vehicles. We ohed and ahed, but couldn't understand what the *señor* was saying half the time because of his lisp. Nor did we know where we were going. Our road turned uphill, and brought us to a school where there was to be a horse show. We parked and the *señor* offered to show us the school grounds. Twelve o'clock was upon us, but he showed us every room. Quite exciting— empty school rooms! He stopped every horse lover in sight and introduced us. Our stomachs were growling as we headed toward the parking lot.

Then to our surprise they cleared the lot and said they'd have the show right there. During the next hour, as rains moved up across the mountain, the field was readied, a running lane set up, a clothesline strung over the lane, ribbons pinned onto the rope, rules agreed upon, money laid down, horses quieted, and finally rider after rider—in almost monotonous succession tried to spear a ribbon with a tiny pick. The horsemen were drinking a lot, so the ribbons were quite safe. Spectators walked around, calling out to each other. The *señor* was pleased with the world. Poor Señora Gutiérrez and her burned Sunday dinner. But the *señor* didn't seem to have her in mind.

Sometime later, after I was about exhausted hushing the kids whose hunger was pretty severe, the *señor* told us to tell him when we were ready to go! We left. When we arrived back at the house I expected a scene between a fiery housewife and a lisping husband. No, there was no war. She wasn't upset in the least. Why should she be, for the dinner wasn't even begun! We finally ate, but by then it was going on four o'clock and the kids had some homework to do and I was tired from the cross-cultural time zones, so I said we should be on our way.

Four o'clock in the afternoon, I wish to insist, is getting pretty late, even though the *señora* called it "early afternoon." To this day, when someone sets an appointment with me for *"la pura tarde"* (literally the pure afternoon), I am at a loss to know when to show up. I usually carry a book with me to pass the time.

From the sidelines, these confusions over *time* can be funny, but on the playing field, they make the difference on whether there will be a fumble or not. Here is a related case, in which *time* contributes to misunderstanding.

Case 11

Jan (in a letter):

Dear Prof. During the final week of our work assignment there is a national holiday on Thursday. And we hear that a lot of people at the places we work will be taking a four-day vacation. So we will effectively terminate our jobs on Wednesday instead of Friday. Would you give us permission to leave town early, so we can take a trip down Rio Sucio to Rio San Juan to the Atlantic, then by canal to Limon? We'll pay all expenses of course, and our host families say it's okay with them.

Sr. Pablo Malavassi:

We are sorry that our North American visitor didn't like it here. She just didn't relate well to the community. Nothing in the town seemed to interest her much. We could tell she was dissatisfied because she left early even though her friends at work were planning a farewell party for her on the final weekend.

Up to this point, we have drawn our cases from the student/family relationship. Let's broaden out a bit to include a wider social circle. There is no better way to begin than to study the *fiesta,* Costa Rica's pastime and national sport. We shall examine two fiestas, a Latin American one and a North American one, and note the responses to each.

Case 12

Mercedes Barrantes, elementary schoolteacher:

The Mother's Day party—what a beautiful occasion. School was crowded from 8 to 2. Everybody was there. Mothers smiling. Children proud of their mothers. Programs. Banners. Food. Do you know that third grade put on a play, and fifth grade actually hired a combo? The whole thing—beautiful. The dances and the flowers.

Mrs. Elizabeth Widdle:

In all my life, I've never seen such bedlam. Never. And spare me of it again. Mass confusion, swarms of people, yelling and screaming, horns and drums. I tried to find Kathy's classroom, and frankly it was a case of total chaos. Even the teacher didn't seem to know what was going on. There was to be a play, yet nobody knew what the play was to be. It needed some improvisations, to be sure. They didn't even know in which part of the room it would be staged. The kids did put something on, but I heard nothing of it thanks to roving troubadours outside. Mothers shouted "Louder! Louder!" but we heard nothing. What was the point of the party?

Case 13

Jason:

I took a break from Latin America on Friday night, went to a party of Gringos, over by Escazu, with a Peace Corp friend. We got into a good discussion there about drug traffic, from Colombia up the Costa Rican coast, through to the States. They say there is a network a bit like the underground railroad that keeps the stuff on the move. First intelligent discussion I've been in since coming here.

Señora Beatriz Madrigal:

We Costa Ricans show our feelings. At a funeral we cry. At a wedding we have a party. We show affection even in public. We get angry and we get happy. All of the emotions we use all the time. So you can understand why I was surprised when I attended a North American party in Escazu. It was like a wake. People introduced each other, "This is my boyfriend," or, "This is my girlfriend," but they showed no affection for each other. People sat in groups and talked only with certain people. All very serious. It didn't seem like a party to me.

We have invited Costa Ricans to visit our classes, to demonstrate certain kinds of unacceptable and acceptable party conduct. It is complex enough to need a how-to-do-it manual!

Case 14

Julio Vargas (Spanish teacher):

The first day of Spanish classes we were receiving a torrential downpour—typical of our tropical afternoons. I arrived at the classroom and there prepared my materials while I waited for my first group of newly arrived North American students. I heard them coming, for they were very noisy. They broke into the classroom without knocking. They were soaked to the skin. They didn't think to carry umbrellas. Then, in the most unbelievable action that I can remember in my years of teaching, they took off their shoes, then their stockings, and at the window squeezed out the water, all the while laughing and babbling. Not once did any of them recognize me, nor even give me a greeting. I thought to myself, "How can I teach such brutes?" But I started talking and they listened as though nothing they did was crude. No one ever apologized for the incident.

No, they didn't apologize and they won't, for if they recall the incident it will be "wreathed in the mystique of adventure, reserved for our grandchildren," as one student wrote in a letter after he returned to the United States.

Just as Professor Vargas was surprised, so the North American is caught off guard by certain Latin American conduct.

Case 15
Arnold Thomas (professor from U.S. in Costa Rica):
  I was invited to give two lectures to a church group which was meeting at a mountain retreat for an entire Saturday. As I expected, my first lecture in the morning was followed by a long period of argument and debate in which everyone seemed completely unaware of anything but his own opinion. I knew the afternoon would go the same way . . . and into the night, so at noon I asked the leader whether I might slip out midafternoon. After my lecture, I remained for about 30 to 45 minutes until the debate was quite hot, then quietly excused myself. Wait one moment! My getting up brought the entire meeting to a standstill. The leader made a long explanation why I had to leave. Then they felt obligated to give me a farewell, which consisted of a closing hymn and prayer, expressions of appreciation from everyone, handshakes all around, and a delegation going with me to the car. I was completely embarrassed, and had I known. I would have stayed til ten o'clock to avoid the scene.

The foreigner has to search for the general principles

that guide the actions of the local native peoples, and hope for some kind of patterns to emerge. What, for example, is the guiding principle in Professor Vargas' annoyance with the students that in turn is the same guiding principle that causes the church people to break up their meeting? An element of time? No. An element of noise? No. Guess and guess again. Permit me to identify the guiding principle. The church people, although they seemed totally absorbed in their debate, were culturally determined to give first attention to human relations. Their guest was leaving; he should be given attention. And so Professor Vargas expected the same attention to human relations, specifically the students' recognition of him the teacher. There is hardly ever a rain that is more important than a teacher, and certainly wet socks are never more important than a teacher. To wring out the water in front of the teacher is anti-recognition.

Such guiding principles can indeed help students make sense out of confounding situations. But in Case 16, Bill can see no sense, because he does not understand a deeper principle.

Case 16

Bill:

The people of this nation are cruel to handicapped persons. In my year here, I've seen grown men teasing a mentally retarded boy. I've seen boys pitching pebbles at an old man who'd rage at them; I've heard people whistling and jeering at homosexuals. Even in private homes, I've seen grandparents teased. To top it off last week at the migration office, a lad went to a window and asked what time the office would close. A bad speech impediment forced him to use *l* instead of *r*. The government clerk responded loudly, mocking the impediment by using an *l* for each *r* in her answer. The office staff laughed.

Carlos Valenciano:
   Bill sees and hears teasing, but he misunderstands it. We
tease everyone here. Everyone whom we like. To be teased
is to be a part of the family. We keep handicapped people in
our homes and treat them like anyone else. Sure, we tease
them in anyway we can. In the United States, you put
handicapped and elderly people away in institutions where
you don't talk at all with them. That is what I would call
cruelty.

   There we have it again, different points of view on
human relations. Different ways to relate to each other.
Within the confines of one's own culture, most of our
social interactions are so nearly automatic that there is
hardly need to consciously interpret what's going on. But
when one finds the automatic responses inappropriate, in
a foreign setting, one wants to ask with Eliot's Prufrock,
"Do I dare to eat a peach" [3]
   The next case pertains to a town whose reputation
nearly caused us to discontinue placing students there.
Clifford summed up our point of view.

Case 17

Clifford:
   My family always wants to drag me out of the house.
Someone says, *"Vamanos a pasear"* and out we go. For
what? Good question. We walk around, then around again,
and for a fresh change, we go the other way around. I've
never seen such an idle bunch of men and boys, sitting in the
park, calling *piropos* to the girls, arguing over soccer games,
playing marbles, *vacilando* as they themselves admit. And
my work assignment has been a zero. Nobody works. The
people sit around, drink coffee, go downtown. What a waste
of human energy.

Raul Benavides, university student:
   My town is the best one in the country. It has a reputation

for being *alegre*. Friendly people, clean air, bright sunshine. We're loafers. We like to fool around in the park, enjoying friends. We have this tradition: parents take their babies to the cathedral for the official christening, but then they go to the park for the town loiterers to give the nickname. We then use the nickname. We're really good at giving nicknames—Cheese, The Shepherd's Crook, Mortar and Pestle, Parrot. I never get my courses completed in a semester because I'm heading toward the university and someone says, "Hey, let's have a coffee" and so we have a coffee. It's a good town and a good life. We all know each other. If you address a letter to me, just the name, care of the town, I'll get it sooner or later.

Our college, fortunately, did not abandon this town, but production-oriented students had to learn how to waste time creatively while in that town. That is, they had to learn how to pass the time by having fun with neighbors.

Of the many forms of social interaction, the one that most dramatically and regularly "exposes" for our students the deep cultural imprint upon human relations is *dating*. How can one pleasantly and comfortably socialize with people of another culture, especially people of the opposite sex, without the burden of embarrassing errors, nagging misunderstandings, or undesirable sexual involvements? The question does not remain an academic one for long, because (1) most university students enjoy dating, (2) Latin American males are perceived to be romantic and aggressive, (3) North American females are perceived to be attractive and liberated, (4) Latin American females are perceived to be interested in gaining North American husbands, (5) North American males are perceived to become goggle-eyed over Latin American *señoritas*, and (6) any *faux pas* in dating rather quickly incites the wrath of the conservers of any culture's traditions. And if you conclude that the six "forces," in concentrated form, make a blast of cultural dynamite, you are correct. Relatively few events of dating among students and local people begin, proceed, and end happily.

Let us "look in" on several cases, the first of which involved two North Americans, and the *señora* of the co-ed.

Case 18

Larry:

I took Barb out last week to a party to which her host sisters invited her. They hardly looked at me, and I know it's because I'm black. Then Barb's *señora* greeted her the next morning with the ridiculous rules that Barb must always ask her permission before having a date, and she must be back at the house by 10 p.m. Who says this country doesn't discriminate against blacks! She has made the rules only to exclude me from their social circle. So I decided to disregard the *señora*. I met Barb in town last night. We stayed out until we were ready to return to the house. Then, to our surprise, the vindictive *señora* wouldn't let Barb into the house. We knocked and knocked until finally she opened the door. Now I hear that Barb must be transferred to another host family.

Sra. Aida de Esquivel:

We do not want this girl in our house, nor anyone else from that program. We are a respected family, and I am an honorable woman. I fully expect my own daughters to follow my pattern. I will not expose them to the lack of respect that both Barbara and her friend displayed. They did not ask me prior to their first outing. They were not friendly to the Costa Ricans at the party. They came home later than an acceptable hour. I only asked Barbara to observe the rules that my own daughters and their good friends obey. Then, after the second violation, when I was good enough to allow

Barbara into the house after midnight, in open disdain and disrespect, the man gave a kiss to the girl there on my veranda in front of me. No, thank you, we shall not have the girl.

Nine o'clock curfews, chaperons, permissions, conversations but no amorous scenes on the veranda, certain etiquette at a party—the dating game has interesting rules in other cultures. I remind students that dating, within the boundaries of one's own culture, can be thoroughly confusing. Why should it be less so in cross-cultural situations?

Case 19

Jean:

My little host cousin made a kind of raft and offered to take me out in the shallow harbor one afternoon. I was glad to go. A couple hundred feet from shore, we pulled close to a nice-looking yacht. A man was sitting in it—I had recognized him but couldn't quite remember where in town I had seen him. He was fixing something at the yacht, and when we called up to him and chatted a bit, he invited us to take a look at his yacht. My little cousin didn't want to leave his raft, and I didn't want to be impolite, so I climbed onto the yacht and looked around while my cousin rowed in the harbor for half an hour or so. He returned, I got onto the raft and we returned to shore. Nothing, absolutely nothing, occurred between the man (who, I learned, is the doctor at the hospital) and me. We simply drank Cokes while he told me about his fishing.

Doña Flora de Bermudez

Earlier I esteemed Jean as different from the other loose North American girls, but now I know differently. She was most indiscrete to accept his invitation. We all know story after story of his exploits, the women, his children. North American girls give their virtue away.

No matter how sincere Jean may be in her account of
the activities, and no matter how diligent she may be in
trying to restore her good reputation, she will likely not
persuade anyone because the first message she sent out
carried to the local people no ambiguities at all. Hers was
an immoral act.

We have discovered that Costa Ricans do not wish to
criticize a person to his/her face, nor to give corrective
counsel. This reserve has been especially true in
questions of dating. Even though a *señora* might feel
strongly about an "indiscretion" involving a North
American guest who is dating, she is likely not to speak
directly about the error. She might, however, speak to
the neighbors!

Case 20

Charlotte:

I could die! Never have I been so embarrassed, yet I must
remain in this town another month. Here's my story. I met a
fellow who struck me as being friendly, decent, considerate.
We talked, met each other on occasions, always behaving as
friends, nothing more. This town has its weekly fiesta at El
Prado on Friday nights. Everybody goes. I went with my
sisters. Music, dancing, something to eat, and drink. The
guy was there and asked me to dance. I don't dance much,
but to be a sport, I accepted. We danced one or two times
that night and the next week. So it went for a month. Now
the bombshell. Steve (another student) came to the house
yesterday to tell me he learned that the whole town is
talking. It's a scandal. Why? That guy is married and has a
family! Now why for heaven's sake didn't my sisters and
mother tell me? I went to my mother right away and her
response was a roundabout, "I thought you knew."

There are times however that people do indeed
"tattle," but that doesn't necessarily make the case easier
for North Americans to understand.

Case 21

Rodrigo Sanabria (in a telephone call to the program leader):

I thought it wise to inform you that Tina will be running off this weekend with a man. We have appreciated her. She is relating nicely at the school of special ed and has made many friends, but this weekend is causing much consternation in her family because she and this man are going alone to Puntarenas. We had not known they were *novios*. As you know, such activity is completely unacceptable here in this town where everyone knows each other. It will of course reflect badly on the school, on her family, and on your program.

Tina:

Yes, I know who called you. Rodrigo Sanabria. It makes me furious. Let me tell my side. The fellow is Jaime Chaverri. You know his family in Heredia—they've hosted many students. Jaime works at the school of special ed. He got his degree last year. You know all this, and probably know him much better than I do. Okay, we have worked together. Then he told me that his family has a cabin by the ocean. He is helping to build it, and goes there every weekend. He asked if I wanted to go sometime and I said yes.

Just in case you are wondering what's going on between us, let me remind you that I am engaged to a guy back home, and fully respect that engagement. I talked to my host family and they said okay. We were planning to leave Saturday morning and get back Sunday afternoon. But now that I know of the talk in town, I told Jaime that I wouldn't go. My story isn't finished. The town judged me—or should I more accurately say that Rodrigo Sanabria judged me—for what were good motives. Who is going to judge Rodrigo Sanabria? Do you know that none other than Rodrigo Sanabria has been a pest ever since I arrived here? He is coaxing, proposing, making all kinds of passes and yet the guy is married. He had the gall to tell me just last week that he'll divorce his wife if only . . .

Case study 21 is likely to stimulate a lot of conversation among North Americans who cannot accept traditional dual-ethics for men and women. The good woman according to such prescriptions is the symbol of purity and divine love, and consequently guards her chastity. The man, on the other hand, is supposedly endowed with urges that must be met. A father may rigorously protect the virginity of his daughter while he maintains a mistress. Such ethics make little sense to most of our students. Nor can the students accept the charge that Tina, and not Rodrigo (as seen by the Latin American), is in charge of her virginity. By going away alone with a man, she is publicly relinquishing that virginity.

Enough on dating. Let us consider *social contracts*. The conventions of interacting that transpire casually do sometimes lead to more formalized contracts. The contracts might not be written on legal paper and signed in the presence of a lawyer. Yet they may, like some insurance policies, have fine print that two people of the same culture fully understand, but that outsiders misunderstand. North Americans "sign" social contracts when they don't know they are doing it, as illustrated in Case 22.

Case 22
Ted Hutchinson:

My kids were on vacation, bored, and therefore bugging each other. So on the spur of the moment I thought, "Gee, why not let them go down to Quepos for the weekend with the Castro family." I called Armando and he was overjoyed at hearing my proposal. The kids went, and had a lovely time. Castros met them at the bus station, planned lots of activities including a picnic to the beach, and sent them back on Monday morning with a box of fresh pineapples.

I hadn't realized how much I had honored them by imposing my kids on them. They were honored that the kids liked them, and they were honored that I had confidence to entrust the kids to them. On the other hand, I didn't know the depths of these new ties between us until don Armando asked me later whether we could take their daughter with us to the States for 6-9 months and entertain her while she brushes up on her English. He is honoring us back and fully expects our reciprocation. But think of the expense and burden!

No wonder that North Americans, fearful of such IOUs, shrink away from involvements. No wonder that Latin Americans, whose social interactions are made possible by such interdependencies, read the North American's reserve as nothing other than personal dislike. In Case 23, a social contract is "signed" when Roger Smith first contacts Guillermo Rojas about a cabin on the coast. What does that contract give to each person? What is expected of each person? Who reneges on the contract? Try to decipher the small print as Latin Americans would read it.

Case 23

Roger Smith:

Great weekend. We parked the car by a cottage (a boy promised to guard it) and then hiked three kilometers to the cabin which sat on the very point that juts into the bay. We were there alone. Nobody but nobody interfered with our weekend paradise. Now that's strange to talk that way. Guillermo Rojas—our company's agent in the town ten kilometers from the point, the guy whom I had asked about the cabin—he walked out there Saturday afternoon, and insisted for an hour that we go along back into town with him to spend the evening. What would we want to do that for? And once he came, it was a bit difficult to get rid of him, but he finally got the point.

Guillermo Rojas:

There they were, sitting alone on the point for a whole

weekend. No people, not even a radio. Nothing. I tried to persuade them to have fun in town. I would have shown them the place, taken them to a party, and even let them stay in my house for the night. But they didn't seem to be very warm. I had even carried some barbecued chicken there, but they didn't express much thanks.

Social contracts bind together two or more people. To many a North American the person who is party to the contract should be distinguished from the terms of the contract. On paper that reads a bit strange, and yet most of us could cite cases where a North American has said, "Now don't take this personally, but let's break it off!" That separation of person from contract terms is strange to the Latin American. To break a contract is likely to move close to a personal offense, and as such calls for a defense of one's own honor. We'll illustrate with Case 24.

Case 24

Ruth:

I was assigned to work in the children's ward and actually looked forward to playing with the kids, and where possible, helping the nurses. To my great disappointment, the assignment was a flop. There were only 5, 6, or 7 babies in the ward—all infants or at least under two years of age—and most of them had bronchial problems. There were three attendants, women, not even licensed practical nurses, who just sat around all day, gossiped and smoked. They seemed to wonder what I was doing there, and of course I did too—15 minutes into my first hour. The eight-hour shift was the longest day I've ever had. So when Margaret said that there was plenty for me to do in the lab, I mentioned it to the attendants, and they thought it okay for me to go down there. They were probably relieved to see me go. I went to the lab and got to work until the supervisor of nurses saw me and blew her top. "Get back to the children's ward," etc., etc. The Spanish really erupted. I cried, I'll admit it, I cried.

If Ruth had only talked it out first with the supervisor of nurses—the person initially responsible for her placement—chances are high that the change would have been made smoothly. Having been by-passed, the supervisor defended her own honor in the following manner:

Doña Raquel Ramirez:
That girl has no sense of shame! What disregard for our hospital services. The *gringos* who insist on coming here to help us poor souls think the place is theirs and that they can do as they please. The agencies think they are doing God a favor to send us the volunteers, but they should know that many of the *gringos* give us a headache. Usually they don't understand Spanish well enough to get along, nor do they know our processes. The last volunteer wasn't here an hour until she was yelling, "Get that insulin into the refrigerator, get that insulin into the refrigerator," as if we didn't know. They are so arrogant.

Earlier we noted that North Americans "sign" social contracts when they don't realize they are signing, and they break contracts when they don't realize they are breaking them. On the other hand, North Americans who have been in our program often assume they are party to contracts with Costa Ricans that the latter do not respect. There is no easier source for case studies than the issue of *personal property*.

Case 25
Robin:
Thievery makes me very angry. Purses are snatched on the streets. Wallets are lifted in buses. Even in my own home, I've lost jewelry. My cosmetics are about gone, and I'm not the one who used them. Money is missing. My bureau drawers are regularly searched as are my suitcases.

My sisters have actually worn my clothing to school. When I think about the low level of morality that allows thievery, I wonder whether there are equally low ethical standards in other areas of life.

What is a social contract to Robin is not a social contract to Professor Joaquin Salas. Notice how this shows up in his response.

Professor Joaquin Salas:

If you don't want your sister to use your cosmetics and jewelry and clothing, lock them. If you don't want your purse snatched, hold it tighter, or fasten a strap to it which you can wrap around your arm. Men shouldn't carry wallets. In summary, you must supply the guard. If we want to protect our cars, we build locked garages. If we want to protect our houses, we build block walls around them, and cover the top of the walls with broken glass. Some people hire night watchmen. We as a family *never* leave our houses unattended, even for 20 minutes. It is our way of doing things: something that is left open in the public view belongs to the public. A cosmetic left on your bureau belongs to the whole family.

To restate this dilemma, the North American sees the whole realm of personal property as material for a social contract: I shall respect your personal property as you respect mine. To the Latin American, the social contract is more person-oriented, while things are literally "up for grabs." (The Latin American visiting rural midwestern United States is impressed with our unlocked doors; the North American upon visiting Latin America, is impressed that everyone carries keys.)

In the following case notice the public response to unguarded property and observe who is blamed for the consequences.

Case 26

Hermana Josefina Fonseca:

We operate the orphanage on will power alone. If we only had some money to go with it! You heard about the "free store?" A month ago when we were desperate for money to repair the roofs, we got government permission to have a duty-free store for a day. We filled a classroom with liquor, cosmetics, small appliances, and foreign gifts. The government said that the clerks at the duty-free store of the airport would have to run it, so they promised to be here at 9 a.m. to begin the sale. At 8 already, the crowds were pounding the doors. Then, for some reason, the clerks didn't come til 2 in the afternoon. They never explained why. The people by nine o'clock couldn't be restrained. They broke in, and because there weren't guards or clerks, they cleaned out the store—even members of the school's executive council helped themselves. We should have had guards, it was our fault.

That the Catholic sister would take the blame for this incident doesn't speak so much of her tolerance and forgiveness but rather her cultural upbringing. Her response strikes us as singularly inappropriate, but we must recognize that our point of view is culturally conditioned. (The Latin American, if pressed, could cite graphic cases of North American greed and theft, which of course, we would justify quite conveniently.)

The cases I have selected for this chapter thus far have illustrated points of view about human relationships. We could go on and on, telling of funny, sad, horrible, dangerous incidents.

—Who pays for the Cokes at the restaurant?
—What does a policeman's whistle mean?
—Who is noisier, a Latin American or the North American?
—Should you accept a glass of water if you think it is contaminated?

—What should you do if people break into the line and get
waited on before you do?
—What should you do if a rooster keeps you awake at night?
—Should a priest give communion to the drunk who is
kneeling at the altar rail beside you?

Such questions can sharpen the attention of newly
arrived foreigners, and begin to sensitize them to the
thousand interesting ways that the host culture expresses
itself differently from one's home culture.

To conclude the chapter, I shall stray from illustra-
tions of human interactions to deal briefly with
points of view about wealth/poverty and development/
underdevelopment. I have selected these areas because
they represent a special stumbling block to international
good will. The colossal ignorance of North Americans
about Third World countries causes educated Latin
Americans to shake their heads in disbelief. North
Americans, given their vast and ubiquitous system of
mass communications, given their years in school, given
their interest in travel, nonetheless know so little about
what's going on in the world! One day as I sat in the San
Jose Union Church (an inter-Protestant association for
English-speaking worshipers) waiting for the service to
begin, the North Americans around me were talking. As I
listened in on one conversation, the words seemed to
amass themselves into a kind of "sense of the world" that I
juxtaposed against another set of words that I had just read
from a brochure released by The Christophers, entitled
Coffee, The Rules of the Game, and You.[4] Let me try to
recreate these two senses of the world; I shall report the
conversation in the column to the left and the brochure in
the column to the right. We might entitle this exercise,
"Do you see what I see?"

Central America according to two business persons in conversation at church

He: I just got in from Cayman Islands.

She: Oh, how was it?

He: We go constantly. We got the price down, so we can cut the bill every time we go. We got land there, and last night they held the plane while Betty got things done at migration.

She: John and I were going to take friends up through Central America on John's next trip. But in mid-September there's to be a nationwide strike in Nicaragua.

He: Apparently something's going on in Salvador too.

She: We like to take friends. While John sees his customers, I show friends the touristy things, but if things aren't settled in Nicaragua . . .

He: Yea, whatever there is in Salvador, I don't know, but something's going on.

Central America according to a brochure with information about El Salvador.

One third of all the wealth and income in El Salvador is concentrated in the hands of 5 percent of the population. A family in this sector receives an annual income 12 times greater than what the poor two-thirds of the people can expect to earn in a year.

One affluent person in El Salvador consumes as much as do 13 of his poorer countrymen.

As the wealthy minority develops more of a taste for consumer goods, it diverts Salvador's financial resources towards the purchase of cars, TV sets, and other items suited to its personal needs and desires.

Tax evasion, fraud, foreign bank accounts, and the misappropriation of government funds often go hand in hand with these concentrations of wealth.

She: They say it won't affect business. John can still see his customers.

He: No, it won't affect business. It hurts the people.

She: They want (President) Somoza out. But think, a nationwide strike—everything shut down.

He: I just don't know what's going on in Salvador. Things are nice in the Cayman Islands. A lot of rain though. I went with a cold, but it's cleared up now.

She: I get colds easily but I take Vitamin C.

He: I take Vitamin C also.

The wealthy one per cent of the agricultural population controls more than 40 percent of the arable land, whereas only 11 percent of the land is shared among the poorer 78 percent of the agricultural population. The poor must either work on the lands of the rich or eke out a living on small, unproductive plots of ground.

It is not uncommon for the ruling groups in countries like El Salvador to denounce as "subversive activities" any effort to alter the rules which ensure the permanence of their privilege.

Two views of Central America! And to take a look at both views while sitting in church! Many students have felt the shock of economic differences, whose tremors have caused students to respond in a variety of ways. Some love to buy cheap goods to take back home. Others are embarrassed by their own wealth. One such student reported a most revealing conversation she had had with her host father, Enrique.

Enrique: You will have to pardon our humble hospitality.

Karen: Humble? I love it here. I feel quite comfortable. You
    are of the middle class, and so am I.
Enrique: But you are rich. Your family is rich.
Karen: No, not at all. We are not rich.
Enrique: What is your father's work?
Karen: My father raises pigs in Illinois.
Enrique: Pigs? Oh.
Karen: I told you we weren't rich.
Enrique: But how many pigs?
Karen (stuttering): Oh, maybe two thousand. Maybe three.
Enrique: Do you have a car?
Karen: Yes, an old 56 Chevy.
Enrique: Is that your only car?
Karen: Uh, we have a 73 Pontiac.
Enrique: Do you have more cars?
Karen: My brother has one and my Dad just got a new
    Pontiac.
Enrique: Do you have trucks?
Karen: Yes, we have a pickup and a straight cattle truck and
    two *semis* for the farm.
Enrique: Tractors?
Karen: Yes, several.
Enrique: Well, you will have to pardon our humble
    hospitality.

It is not an uncommon reaction of North Americans to
flinch at poverty, then to pity the impoverished people,
but ultimately to complain about impoverishment because it causes personal inconvenience. A language
teacher of mine said, "When I ask the class to tell me
about my country, the comments are usually negative."
For example, the road to the coast is perceived by the
coastal dweller as a link to the capital, cheap and rapid
transit, a chance for a holiday, the privilege of traveling
with friends, beautiful scenery. To the North American,
the road is bad, the holes deep, the trip four hours long,

the passengers motion sick, the driver careless.

The North American's point of view may at times be guided by strictly selfish desires—such as personal comfort—which may effectively blind him/her to the more objective reality. That is, I may be so concerned about my health, my happiness, my fortunes that I cannot see beyond my near environment. Following Costa Rica's recent national elections in which a variety of fundamental issues were debated at length, a crusty North American published his suggestions for the new president's immediate agenda. His list included:

- —Don't let there be water shortages.
- —Set up public toilets.
- —Prohibit spitting on the floor.
- —Get beggars off the streets.

It is easy for me to be caustic about such narrow-mindedness, yet I myself am frequently reminded of my own eclipses of vision. One day I decided to kill ten minutes downtown by getting my shoes shined in Parque Central. After all, it cost only 25 cents. A grimy old man asked for the job and I consented. After he began his work, I thought, "I know what that guy looks like from this angle. What do I look like from his angle?" So we got to talking, and I learned that

- —He was father of eight children.
- —He worked from 6:00 a.m. til 5:00 p.m. or until the rains came.
- —On a good day, he could earn $4.00 but usually he took home no more than $3.00.
- —At home, he'd try to augment his income by repairing shoes.

—He went "on the drunk" every month or two.
—He was kind to me, and asked about my family.

He shined my shoes particularly well. They almost became a mirror, revealing me as, yes, a rich North American whose impressions . . . .

CHAPTER
TWO

Encounters

A theoretical model explaining the
dynamics of cross-cultural communication

Successful Foreigners

Among those hundreds of thousands of persons who live abroad, which ones are the successful foreigners?

If we were to ask the foreigners themselves to answer the question, we would likely hear from most of them a testimonial of high adventure. What reveals success better than the good story? For example, Sancho Panza, upon his return with Don Quixote from a trip through La Mancha and into the Sierra Morenas, says to his wife:

I can tell you one thing by the way, namely, that there's nought in this world so pleasant as for an honest, decent man . . . on the prowl for adventures. 'Tis true, I must say, that most we knocked up against were not so comfortable as a body would wish, for out of a hundred that we met, the ninety-nine usually fell out cross and crooked. I know by experience, but when all's said and done, it's a fine thing to be gadding about spying for chances, crossing mountains, exploring woods, climbing rocks, visiting castles, lodging at inns at our own sweet will . . . [1]

If we were to decide which of the foreigners were successful on the basis of their reputations after they returned home, we'd have to say that most would have been successful, because it seems that since Odysseus' triumphant return to Ithaca, anybody who ventures abroad and then arrives home safely "has it made." There is status in having been a foreigner. Richard P. Coleman and Lee Rainwater, in their analysis of the American "status quotient" in *Social Standing in America*,[2] claim that "the most envied use of money is for travel and expensive recreation." It is reported that a child, after seeing the warm welcome given a missionary upon the latter's return to the United States, announced that when she grew up she wanted to be a returned missionary.

When we try to answer the question, "Who is the successful foreigner?" through more objective measures, we often make our evaluations on the basis of the foreigner's original objective in going overseas. Was the college degree that she sought in Germany finally obtained? Did the cattle ranch on the Chaco produce a profit? Were the relief funds for Bangladesh distributed? Did the new church in Botswana add members?

But "success by objective" may conceal as much as "success by testimonial." Just because the bottom line looks good, one can't always judge the processes that led to the results of the bottom line. I have known people who met their objective in going abroad, and who carried extraordinary reportage and good slide transparencies along home, who nonetheless were unmitigated failures on foreign terrain where they hated every unending hour of every unending day. Even dear Sancho Panza gave a positive testimonial when only one in a hundred adventures turned out well!

I am suggesting in this chapter that there is another element in the definition of successful foreign living that most of us, strange as it may seem, generally tend to overlook. *How effective is the foreigner in relationships with local native peoples?*

The issue of day-to-day relationships is concealed from the people back home, not intentionally perhaps, but concealed nonetheless. "The natives" seldom impress us beyond some stereotypes. It was in church, rather than in the town hall, the theater, or the school where some of us got our first and strongest impression of "the natives." We church folk were sufficiently acquainted with phrases such as "the sick," "the dying," "the heathen," "the lost" that when missionaries showed their pictures of black Africans looking at the camera, Indians washing in the Ganges, Latin Americans in a fevered dance on the saint's day, or hungry orphans in crowded shanty towns, we accepted as a stereotyped reality "the teeming millions." There were songs about taking "the gospel of light to the lands that are wrapped in the darkness of night." Such images of "the natives," although powerful, could not make us understand what it would be like to actually talk with them. (I eventually learned about the real thing when missionaries brought to the home churches some of the "converts" and I discovered that after the greeting, it was nigh impossible to think of anything to talk about!)

Every once in a while, the "problem" of relationships is revealed to us, but we don't always catch the significance of the words. For example, the Los Angeles Times Service released a news feature[3] about Americans who went abroad to live, but returned shortly "having discovered the grass is no greener over there." The story quotes Margaret James who went with her family to

Australia "in pursuit of a better life":

> It was terrible; I was cold more often than I ever was in
> Detroit, I can still remember that awful musty smell to
> everything, and we all worked harder than we ever had in
> our lives—and got nothing but the barest survival in return.

Edith Ostrow who went with her husband to Israel:

> Joseph (her husband) had his work. But I spoke no
> Hebrew. I was in my late 50s and I was partially blind in one
> eye. I was very lonely. . . . But mostly it was the laundry. It
> became a symbol. After a few months, I believed that
> happiness in this world amounts to one thing only—owning
> an automatic washer.

Royce Davis who followed his money to El Salvador
where he invested in a construction business:

> I knew I could live like a king there—and I did. . . . Just
> the fact that I'm 6 feet 4 inches tall and the average guy there
> is 5 feet 5 made me feel terrific. . . . You can take your
> Yankee dollars down and actually own people who have
> nothing.

Davis lost his money "through simple, stupid misman-
agement" but never thought of staying on:

> And get some puny little job, for maybe $300 a month and
> live like they do? Ha.

We may read such statements, and we may even
recognize that yes, there are daily problems to be solved
in international living, yes one has to "meet the natives,"
yes one has to learn a foreign language, yet few of us on
home territory ever comprehend the reality of it all.
Finally when some of us do become foreigners, we

discover that interpersonal communication is a challenge
of immense proportions. What we might have accomplished at home now takes superhuman effort. I
myself have rehearsed during a sleepless night the
conversation I faced with the mechanic whom I would ask
to repair the needle of the temperature gauge in my
Toyota, which always showed hot, and although the
mechanics usually reversed the gauges to make C mean
caliente (or hot), this gauge was clearly malfunctioning
because when the motor did indeed heat up, the needle
did not head over toward H. (If you think that
explanation's difficult, try it in faltering Spanish!)

The challenge doesn't go away . . . ever. A person who
becomes a foreigner after age 15 is always a foreigner.

What, then, are the typical responses of foreigners to
this challenge? It's a sad fact that many foreigners
maintain minimal contact with local people. One day,
shortly after our arrival in Costa Rica, I answered a
newspaper ad for used furniture. The directions took me,
to my surprise, to the home of a Protestant missionary.
Our conversation soon touched on language, and here is
what this United States foreigner in Costa Rica told me:

> Language? I give God the glory for what I've got. When I
> was in language school, I was having trouble. So one night
> there in the apartment in San Pedro I prayed, "God, I'm in
> trouble. You saved me, You sanctified me, You called me to
> be a missionary, and You sent me to Costa Rica. Now Satan
> has thrown Spanish in the way. That's an unfair roadblock,
> Lord. I'll make a deal, Lord. If You help me to preach in
> Spanish, I don't care about the rest, like conversation. Just to
> preach. I love to preach the gospel." And you know, God
> answered my prayer. I can preach and although I've got an
> accent, the congregation can understand. That's all I need.
> The Spirit does the rest.

While some people avoid conversation with local people, others retreat into safety zones of fellow-foreigners, kinds of immigrant "ghettos" that effectively seal off the threatening world. Still others intermix with "the natives" but with a brashness and chauvinism that reinforces the ugly-American stereotype.

Who is the successful foreigner? Let me propose a tentative definition. *A person who attempts, with measures of achievement, to create common union with the host peoples of the country he/she is visiting.* Such are the encounters we shall now analyze in more detail.

A Communication Model

When a person in a foreign land first stumbles, he or she impulsively reaches for first aid. It's interesting to notice what kinds of things foreigners try to rely on. Some people use *dollars* to buy their way out of difficulty. Others, particularly from the United States, flash their *passports* or flout their *national identity*. To others, things are changed through prayer.* I've even known people to think that misunderstandings could be solved by *talking louder*! All of us use first aids to help us over the initial culture shock, yet these first aids are likely not to help us understand and develop cross-cultural communication.

For those people who want to be successful foreigners, there is help. Many good books from anthropologists and linguists and community development experts are available in bookshops. Agencies who send people abroad—be they missionary societies or government offices—sponsor training sessions. Relatively few foreign capitals would not have pastors, priests, or professional

---

*I do not wish to imply that prayer is ineffective. See pages 82-83.

counselors to help a foreigner struggling in cross-cultural difficulties. There is help if one looks. The larger difficulty is that some people in trouble don't wish to look for help.

In this chapter I would like to channel some resources of communication theory into this topic of successful foreign living. Communication theory is a form of science, in which investigators try to explain how communication works. Often these investigators begin at a highly abstract level and work their way down out of the clouds and onto the ground of our practical experience. At that abstract level, the communicologists use "models" to represent a simple, schematic form of the complex happening of real life.

I will proceed in the following manner:

1. Introduce one particular model of interpersonal communication.

2. Allow the model builder to explain, in somewhat abstract form, how communication is likely to function. In the telling, he will use a number of important concepts, and indicate essential relationships.

3. Apply the model and its explanations to our topic of successful interaction between a foreigner and native resident.

Let me frankly admit to choosing a model for this occasion in which communication is seen as an act of two people who come to the act from different frames of references, or if you will, from two different points of view.

Back in 1955 Theodore M. Newcomb[4] a social psychologist, proposed a model of person-to-person communication that has endured during an era when such theories lasted about as long as the daily newspaper. His model has become something of a classic, although I have never seen it applied to the cross-cultural context.

Dr. Newcomb put his plow down into this terrain, convinced of two assumptions: First, the elusive and baffling field of social behavior can be understood much more easily by studying particular acts of communication. For example, the all-inclusive problem of foreign living may perhaps be understood better by studying specific communication acts between a foreigner and a native resident.

Second, just as the observable forms of certain chemical solids are macroscopic outcomes of tiny molecular structure (for example, the shape of a crystal corresponding at that big level to its arrangements of molecules), so certain observable social group characteristics may be predetermined by the conditions and consequences of communication acts. Newcomb seems to be saying that the conditions in which businessman Robert Richardson relates in word and action with neighbor Said Abdul Mohammed, and the outcomes of those communicative acts, will go a long way toward determining the larger characteristics of the United States—Somalia social group relationships in the city of Mogadiscio.

Let us look, then, at the model which Newcomb labels "The AtoBreX System." (Read it "the A to B concerning X system.") Consider Missionary Andrew (A) in one of two possible conditions: the state of noncommunication or the state of communication. Also consider his neighbor, Bernardo (B), with whom Missionary Andrew might or might not be in communication. Finally consider the odds and ends (Xs) that Missionary Andrew and Neighbor Bernardo could possibly communicate about. Now let us draw two arrangements, the first showing noncommunication between Missionary Andrew and Neighbor Ber-

nardo, and the second showing communication between
them.

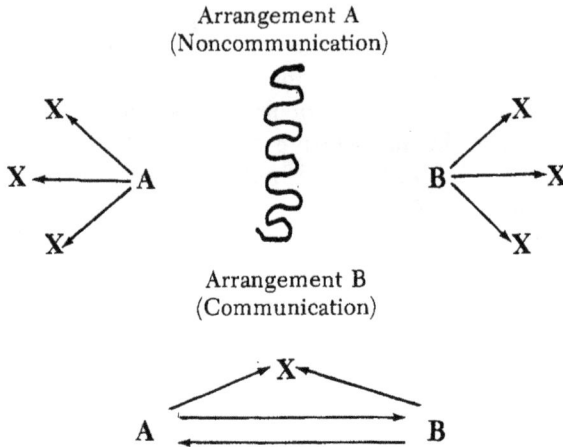

Arrangement A
(Noncommunication)

Arrangement B
(Communication)

The second of the two arrangements depicts Newcomb's AtoBreX system, because Missionary Andrew
interacts with Neighbor Bernardo about something.

Note several things about the state of communication:

1. Andrew has an "orientation" with Bernardo (A:B).
2. Andrew has an "orientation" toward an X (A:X).
3. Bernardo has an "orientation" toward an X (B:X).
4. Bernardo has an "orientation" with Andrew (B:A).
5. Bernardo has an "orientation" toward the same X (B:X)
that involves Andrew (A:X).
6. A and B and X are in "co-orientation" yet each is
independent of others. In being linked, they become a
system. When A communicates to B about X, the system is
functioning.
7. It is possible for Andrew to like Bernardo (+A:B) or to
dislike him (−A:B).

8. It is possible for Bernardo, in turn, to like Andrew (+B:A) or to dislike him (−B:A).

9. Similarly, it is possible for Andrew to have a positive attitude toward X(+A:X) or a negative one (−A:X) and Bernardo can have a positive attitude (+B:X) or negative one (−B:X).

We have been introduced to several important components in this system: *interaction* between *two participants* by way of their simultaneous *orientation* toward some *object of communication* which they may *like or dislike.* Only when there is "co-orientation" between A and B concerning an X can there be communication within this system.

Newcomb would next want us to consider several characteristics of the system. First, this system is not a strange, improbable notion. Co-orientation is essential to life. Andrew can not avoid Xs, unless he is locked up in a dark cell. Life "occurs" as we relate to objects of communication. Neither can Andrew avoid other people unless he is in solitary confinement. What this model clearly indicates, however, is that participants in communication and objects of communication must be brought together into one act. That is, Andrew can't communicate with a person like Bernardo unless there are Xs to communicate about. And just because Andrew has strong feelings about an X doesn't mean that he is communicating about them. He needs a fellow participant.

Second, Newcomb would want us to notice that in his system—as well as in life—there can be agreement (symmetry) in how Andrew and Bernardo view one particular X, or there can be disagreement (dissymmetry). The possible variables can be shown in code form:

−A:X and +B:X	−dissymmetry
+A:X and −B:X	−dissymmetry
−A:X and −B:X	−symmetry
+A:X and +B:X	−symmetry

Let us illustrate symmetry and dissymmetry. We will suppose that Missionary Andrew and Neighbor Bernardo get to talking about the bordering country to the east—which is the perpetual enemy of Bernardo's country. Says Bernardo, "Those Cordobans are less cultured than we are." Andrew thinks a minute and wants to be in accord with his neighbor, so he says, "I find its capital really hot and dirty." Both Bernardo and Andrew have communicated negative attitudes toward an X, and therefore enjoy symmetry. But now suppose that Andrew doesn't feel like being diplomatic, having become somewhat tired of the constant deprecations of the neighboring country, so he bluntly says, "But wait a minute, Bernardo. The Cordobans' rate of literacy is higher than this country's." In code language, Bernardo would have communicated −B:X and Andrew would have communicated +A:X, which would have yielded dissymmetry.

Third, Newcomb says that this system is blessed or cursed with an invisible hand that reaches from the outside into the system. Sounds metaphysical, doesn't it! Newcomb's concept of an invisible hand is just another way to say that there are forces at work to affect the functioning of the system: forces to make A want to relate to B, forces to make A want to disassociate from B, forces to make A want to have a positive attitude toward X, forces to make A want to have a negative attitude toward X. There are many ordinary ways of saying this same thing.

People, for some unexplained reason, are attracted by some people and repelled by others. People gravitate toward some issues, and shrug their shoulders at others. What Newcomb would wish to underscore is that *if* Andrew has a strong desire to relate to Bernardo, and *if* Andrew and Bernardo eventually achieve symmetry toward a common X, Andrew gets important psychological and social and philosophical and physical rewards. In other words, people enjoy friendship.

Fourth, the stronger the force of the invisible hand urging symmetry between Andrew and Bernardo, the more probable that communication between them will bring about symmetry. That principle can be documented with a thousand cases daily: the "kiss-and-make-up" scenes between two fighting kids won't amount to much if the two don't really like each other. On the other hand, a love-spat between two people very much attracted to each other will most likely be resolved when they get together to "talk it out."

And finally, Newcomb's system may be said to be at rest in any one moment. But whenever there is a change in one part, then there must be corresponding reactions in the other parts. Let us say that Andrew and Bernardo, still somewhat strangers to each other, have on occasion exchanged greetings in the early morning when each goes to the *pulperia* to buy bread and milk. We'll let bread and milk be an X. The AtoBreX system is at rest. One morning Andrew enters the *pulperia* just as Bernardo is leaving, after having bought the last two cartons of milk. "Oh, here take this one," says Neighbor Bernardo, "We need only one carton." Andrew accepts. The AtoBreX system has undergone a change. Had Bernardo seen Andrew coming, and finding only two cartons left, had bought them both and walked out grinning maliciously, then again the AtoBreX system would have undergone a change.

There we have it. Newcomb's AtoBreX system of person-to-person communication. But we've only begun our consideration of the model. Let us, like an auto mechanic, now lift up the hood and take a closer look at the works. Later, we will be equipped with sensitized eyes and ears to perceive new dynamics between the foreigner and the native resident.

Ten Postulates

After thinking about his new model, Newcomb had the confidence to say in effect, "Let me guess at what happens in the co-orientation of Andrew and Bernardo, and you see if these guesses of mine do not in fact describe rather accurately a wide variety of situations of interpersonal communication."

Such guesses are called "postulates" in the language of the scientist. A good scientist will then begin making tests to see whether the postulate really holds up. In this section of the chapter, I shall present a sampling of ten postulates (there are many more) by (a) expressing each postulate in code form, (b) putting the idea into lay language, and (c) relating an "incident" that illustrates the validity of the postulate. Our good Missionary Andrew and his Neighbor Bernardo beg off now, so we'll look around for other talent. We shall not discuss the implications of each postulate here, because the next section of the chapter will incorporate such reflections.

Postulate 1

   (a) The stronger the force toward interaction of A to B, the more A will strain for symmetry with BreX.

(b) A friend's attractiveness makes you want to agree with him.

(c) Professor Bancroft, on leave from Columbia State University, is teaching chemistry for a year at the University of Central America. It's been a good year, mainly because of the warm friendships he has established at the university, and particularly in the science departments. The year has brought its surprises. For example, he was outspoken in opposition to the Panama Canal treaties prior to coming, but after being around new friends and hearing them talk, his opinion has softened considerably.

Postulate 2

(a) If a co-orientation with a desirable B is contingent upon a certain A:X, the valence of A:X increases

(b) A person's ability to take bitter medicine depends partially on who's watching.

(c) Arlene Richardson is struggling to adjust to a small dusty provincial city of Chorotega. It wasn't her wish to go there, but Firestone transferred her husband . . . . She put the kids into a private Methodist school, and now Arlene fears she will waste away unless she makes a friend. The best prospect is Teresa Gonzalez, mother of some playmates at school. But the only way of making friends with doña Teresa is to attend those terrible afternoon teas, sponsored by the mother's auxiliary for the school.

Arlene dislikes the gossip, the social maneuvering of the women, and the sweet desserts, but it looks pretty certain that Teresa comes in a package with the teas! Teresa would make a good friend, really . . .

Postulate 3

(a) If a desirable A:B is contingent upon A's perception of B:X, then A is motivated to inform himself of B's orientation and possibly even to change B's orientation to X.

(b) Through all sorts of indirect inquiry, a person will "psych out" a stranger before becoming his friend.

(c) The North American Fruit Company is threatened by a

workers' strike on the plantations and docks. As usual, such events bring tension into the home of the manager of the fruit company. The manager's wife, more than any member of the family, feels the brunt of emotion, because the nastiest rumors are spilled out carelessly whenever the women congregate by the company swimming pool late afternoons. The only ones admitted, by the way, are members of families from the United States or families whose father is in upper management. The women talk—and that talk is vicious. It has been bad enough to cause her to stay away from the pool. Now, it happens that a new family has moved into the administrative "zone" from another zone and as is the custom for the manager's wife, she makes a "welcome wagon" courtesy call. The new *señora* seems to be very nice, but the manager's wife holds her distance. What will this new woman say about the strike, particularly about the hearsay from the other zone from which they came? What is her attitude about labor unions? communist infiltrators? What has she heard about the manager? She steers the conversation carefully around the topic, listening ever so carefully for hints of the new *señora's* attitudes. She'd like to show the new *señora* the other side. How nice it would be to have a friend who'd chose to spend afternoons with her, rather than at the pool where the unkind innuendos cut at self-confidence and trust.

Postulate 4

(a) If +A:B but −B:A, A may seek out other Xs for increasing the attractiveness of B:A.

(b) Children and adults alike employ all sorts of enticements and seductions to gain the attention of possible friends.

(c) I shall not soon forget the visit of an office employee and his family shortly after we arrived in San Jose. He wanted our friendship badly (through us, he wanted a recommendation to get a visa to enter the U.S.). He may have sensed our reserve, for he arrived at the house prepared to attract us . . . if not with one thing, then another. His gifts included a pineapple, two liters of ice cream, four bottles of beer, a bag of caramel candy, and a bar of Chilean copper!

Postulate 5

(a) If A and B are not attracted to each other, but still maintain a co-orientation, the strain toward symmetry is limited to those particular Xs required by the conditions of association.

(b) Two people, who don't like each other much but who are forced by circumstances to have to relate to each other, will make little attempt to agree on anything beyond those items essential for their relationship.

(c) A North American couple lives on 18th street in a South American city. They have the slightest of relationships with the neighbors. Unfortunately they don't talk to each other, they belong to different social circles, the children attend different schools, they represent different fields of employment, different religions, different races. And there is a language barrier. In only one thing MUST they relate: their houses are owned by the same man, who installed a parking garage between the two houses. Both families use the two-car facility; both enter and leave by the same gate; both carry keys to the gate. There are rules to their "relationship." No parking in front of the gate. Park as far to the side of the garage as possible, so two cars can fit. Lock the gate.

Postulate 6

(a) If A and B actively dislike each other, they may use their dissimilar attitudes toward Xs to further disassociate them-selves from each other.

(b) When things come between people, it's easy to look for more grievances.

(c) Mary stayed in the home of the Benavides family for six months when she was spending her junior year in Honduras. She was supposed to stay for a full year, but "things came between them." It started when Mary walked out of the house after an argument over the hour she should be in at night. Her family said ten o'clock ("We're a respectable family") and Mary said she was old enough and responsible enough to make her own decisions. They couldn't agree; Mary left. But if you'd talk with Mary or the Benavides family now, you'd get your ears burned. According to Mary, the father is autocratic and impulsive, the brother stole her money, the 11-year-old sister is spoiled, the mother is always fussing about homemade health remedies. The Benavides family says that Mary did not bathe daily, seldom said thank you, frequently retired to her room without entering into family activities, was picky in her eating, and seemed not to make a good attempt to learn the Spanish language.

Postulate 7

(a) The stronger A's attitude about X, the more force there will be toward symmetry with B:X, assuming +A:B.

(b) When a person feels strongly about something, he'll want his best friends to feel strongly about it too.

(c) As a missionary, David feels strongly that personal salvation by Jesus Christ will lead a new convert to a new lifestyle. And so Antonio is causing David some grief. A month ago, Antonio experienced what seemed to be a dramatic religious turnaround, and asked to become a member of the church. But David sees him smoking occasionally. David's children brought home the rumor that he still goes dancing at the night club. And he was seen leaving Bar Isabel just several nights ago. David has preached regularly on the new life in Christ, but without effects upon Antonio. David will have to talk it out with Antonio. Either Antonio changes, or he will be refused membership.

Postulate 8

(a) If A:X is contingent upon an A:B, the valence of A:B increases.

(b) If, to get what you want, you have to get along with a certain person, you can make yourself get along with that person.

(c) Betty Minear accepted a two-year assignment teaching music in a Latin American private school. There, she was invited to be the music director of the large Baptist church that was founded 75 years ago. She accepted enthusiastically, not giving sufficient thought to the sharp contrast between her own love of classical music, cantatas, chorales, and hymns, and the congregation's fondness for fast-moving, hand-clapping *coritos*.

Betty decided upon a compromise. She'd let them have their *coritos* if she could get her one chorale into each Sunday morning service. There's only one hurdle to jump. Jose Antonio, whom Betty finds to be overbearing, gave an electric guitar to the church, and seems to dominate the musical interests of the congregation. Betty will never get her chorale unless she can learn to put up with Jose Antonio and even to gain his friendship and confidence. So far, they are as distant from each other as a chorale is from a *corito*. But Betty scolds herself and stops to chat with him after the service.

Postulate 9

(a) If A:X demands that A be knowledgeable of B:X, A is motivated to find out about B:X.

(b) Sometimes peer group pressures are such that it's good to find out the right opinion on something before putting your foot in your mouth.

(c) The Anderson children, foreigners in Venezuela, are trying to "belong" in school. Particularly Chrissie, 12 years old, is very conscious of her social standing with other girls such as Katia. So when the Spanish kids at school ask Chrissie how she likes the new TV program called *Los Aguaceros* she gives an indefinite answer until she learns that Katia thinks the program *"pura vida."* Then she too says it's one of the best programs she's seen.

Postulate 10

(a) The likelihood of increased symmetry as a consequence of communicative acts increases with attraction and with intensity of attitude.

(b) The more you like her, and the more deeply you feel about this topic, the more likely that you and she will eventually see the topic similarly by talking it out.

(c) Maria Pilar, a pretty and popular university student in Colombia, falls in love with an International Voluntary Service worker from North America who moved to her town. He's handsome, well mannered, intelligent, and rich. To add to her ecstasy, she knows that he likes her. But there is one thing Maria Pilar can't understand. This guy does not dance, nor does he enjoy dancing. He has said that dancing is less than respectable in his social circles back home. He'd rather chat, or play table games, or go for a walk. To Maria Pilar, the weekend dance is a family tradition. Everybody dances. How could she ever give up dancing? There are three alternatives: to discontinue dancing, to convince him to change his mind, or to agree to disagree. But not to give him up!

Before we move into a discussion of what these postulates "say" about the relationship of the foreigner to the native resident, I want to restate that the ten postulates were selected from out of many possibilities. Theodore Newcomb hinted at several additional ways of using his model to generate postulates. I will mention two of those.

All of the postulates I selected referred to Xs as "something to communicate about." But let us change that definition a bit to allow an X to be a role that people play. Imagine for a moment a character named Andres who is *always* joking. He plays the role of comedian. We will let X = the role of comedian. One day he comes upon a friend downtown and is about to tell a joke, when he sees that his friend is crying. The friend's sister, he learns, has become quite ill. Now Andres, because of his relationship with (and respect for) his friend, modifies his traditional role. Newcomb says that one can apply many postulates to Xs as roles.

Furthermore, the AtoBreX system may be modified to include more people: AtoBtoCreX. Imagine the complexities A must work through to enjoy symmetry with B and C, if B and C aren't very close friends. (It's like entertaining in-laws from both sides of the family!) And yet we handle such situations all the time. A-B-X systems may be used to analyze such communicative acts.

Symmetry

The careful study of a communication model, such as Newcomb's, gives to us a new vantage as well as a new vocabulary to answer the question, "Who is the successful foreigner?" I should like to answer that question by rephrasing the tentative definition on page 38:

> The successful foreigner is a communicator who, through interaction with native residents, has enjoyed the rewards of symmetry.

Alas, many foreigners have never aspired to symmetry with native residents. The hippy goes abroad "to find himself." The businessman goes abroad to make money. The student, to get a degree. The tourist, to snap some remarkable pictures. The soldier, to kill the enemy. One might even find Christian missionaries who expect to maintain friction with "the heathen," for as Jesus Himself said, "Blessed are ye, when men shall revile you, and persecute you, and shall say all manner of evil against you falsely, for my sake."

An adventure in international living doesn't have to include native residents. And frankly, to intermix with "the natives" is a bother: let the maid answer the door; let a runner do the local buying; let a private vehicle make bus rides unnecessary; let a Union Church give us our kind of worship; let a club provide us our social fulfilments; let the *International Herald Tribune* keep us informed; let Indiana University's correspondence program educate us.

Fortunately, there are successful foreigners. In one of the loveliest books of the Bible, the aged Naomi who is grieving over the death of her husband and two sons, tells

her daughters-in-law, both foreigners, to return to their
homelands. Why should they remain? Their husbands
had died. So one of the daughters-in-law, Orpah,
returned to her people, but Ruth would not leave. She
said to her mother-in-law; "Where you go, I will go, and
where you stay, I will stay. Your people shall be my
people, and your God my God. Where you die, I will die,
and there I will be buried." I suppose that Theodore
Newcomb enjoys that quotation!

Can you imagine the screening committee of foreign
appointees for a mission board or multinational company
or government agency stipulating that candidates "must
display evidence of genuinely wanting to empathize with
native residents"?

The Participants in Cross-cultural Communication

In any communicative act, the two or more participants
are all-important. We should carefully study what each of
the participants brings to the communicative act.

Each has culturally produced idiosyncracies. I would
guess that if an analyst studied conversations between a
North American and a Latin American . . .

> —the Yankee would talk louder, the Latin American faster.
> —the Yankee would use his head, the Latin would use his heart.
> —the Yankee would talk with his status, the Latin with his hands.
> —the Yankee would be "honest," the Latin would be "convincing."
> —the Yankee would watch the clock, the Latin would watch the face.
> —the Yankee would guard his distance, the Latin would guard his honor.

Each has culturally shaped preferences. I think it safe to assert that most natives of the United States would prefer to be friends with someone from northern Europe rather than from southern Europe. For that majority, Ireland would be a nicer place to visit than Nicaragua. A Japanese guest would be more welcomed than a person from Zaire. So one could "type" any people's preferences.

Each reveals culturally induced attitudes. Many North Americans feel superior to Latin Americans — superior in health, wealth, education, skill, appearance, and general well-being. And North Americans, though they may deny it, do not find the Latin American personality as comfortable to relate to as the European personality. A veteran missionary-educator to Latin America once said to me candidly and with a twinge of remorse, "I must admit I didn't really care for 85 percent of those people, and I hate to fake it. I mean 'care' in the sense of wanting to visit with them."

Each sees through culturally constructed frames of reference. A mother from Wisconsin traveling in southeastern Spain wants to buy a quart of fresh pasteurized homogenized 2 percent milk for today's breakfast cereal. The shopkeeper doesn't understand the request. He has canned milk, shipped in from the northwest provinces. Cereal? At breakfast one eats bread, spread with a bit of olive oil, and drinks coffee with sweetened condensed milk.

For a person to achieve symmetry with others in a cross-cultural setting requires a humble recognition of one's own cultural identity as well as a selfless, courageous acceptance of the other person's cultural identity. That requirement sometimes isn't enough: those of us whose ethnocentrism, nationalism, or regionalism leaves us

handicapped with chauvinistic arrogance will have to deal
with those handicaps immediately.

Patterns of Interaction Between Foreigner
and Resident

Interaction between two participants in communication may take many forms: speech, physical gestures,
facial expressions, writing, greetings, gift giving, and
others.

A person's first venture from his own native culture into
a foreign culture most likely begins in a lack of interaction
(non-orientation) with the strangers of that culture. There
may be a travel agent at the airport ready to slip a wreath
over the visitor's head, or acquaintances who may give a
first night of free lodging, but we won't count those kinds
of contacts as interaction with the local residents. One's
first experiences can be memorable, but brutal. On one of
our family's trips abroad (Spain, 1973-74) we purposely
decided not to structure our first month. We did not write
ahead; we did not know where we'd live; we had not
selected the city, province, or region of our new home.
That month would deserve many pages: finding a glass of
boiled water, getting a car light repaired, trying in vain to
cash a traveler's check, rationing bread because the bank
had not received the money wired from a correspondent
bank in the States and would not extend a loan until the
wire arrived.

One can't survive long totally disassociated from other
people. One must get into orientation with others. But
orientation itself isn't the end of the problem for a
foreigner. At the moment in which a foreigner links up
with a local resident over some subject, chances are high
that the orientation will not achieve instant symmetry. If

you will permit another personal report: I remember our family's first domestic problem in another country. We arrived at our rented house, but there were no clothes hangers in it. Where should we put our clothes? One doesn't live out of suitcases for two years. Where might we find hangers? Whom should we ask? And what should we ask for? The dictionary wasn't much help. I didn't think it appropriate to go out to the barefoot *peon* who was cutting the grass with a *machete,* and ask, "Where can I get a *soporte colgante* or a *colgadero* or a *barra* or a *plancha* or a *hierro de suspensión para ropa."* And when I walked downtown to shop for hangers, I couldn't find any, nor did store clerks know what I was asking for.

After a while, the foreigner's interaction improves (although he may not find clothes hangers to his liking) to the point of being able to make wishes known. (I think that the first irregular verb that gringos learn in Latin America is *querer* — to want.) But it would be an exaggeration to say that the interaction becomes as natural as back home. If you learn the language word by word, you still haven't mastered it. For example, the gringo adds adverbs and adjectives to make things bigger. The Costa Rican adds endings to make things smaller. The Englishman says "black and white," but most of the Spanish speakers I've heard prefer to say "white and black." I have always said "odds and evens," but my neighbors prefer "evens and odds." You flip a coin "heads or tails" don't you. They do it "tails or heads." "Sooner or later" you'll catch on. Or "later or sooner." Such trivial confusion points warningly to the larger barriers to understanding.

Language barriers are merely one kind of wall that separates people of different cultures. Think of the colors of skin, the slant of eyes, height, weight, speed, emotion—things that make people different from each other. Then add to that the cultural rivalries, the immigration quotas, the border skirmishes, the protective tariffs, the diplomatic breaks, the passports and visas, the guards—all of the paraphernalia of antagonistic colonies on our one small planet. The implications of cultural disassociation prompted Professor L. John Martin to state, "Communication occurs only within a culture, since culture defines and patterns our experiences, and these, in turn, control the development of our constructs." He doesn't stop with that discouraging assertion, but shows how people of two disparate cultures can construct a "common culture" by following "common rules of social interaction, of perceiving things in the same way, of organizing one's environment similarly."[5]

Martin's opinion is echoed by Gerhard Maletzke of the Asian Mass Communication Research and Information Center in Singapore: "The extent to which individuals or groups understand one another, fail to understand, or misunderstand, is determined by the degree to which the world views and frames of reference of the partners in communication overlap."[6]

The reader can readily detect a negative, discouraging tone to this discussion of interaction between foreigner and resident: disassociation, nonorientation, dissymmetry, language barriers, cultural disparities, nonintersecting frames of reference. It sounds quite bad, indeed. And it could be made to sound worse, if we told stories of poeple who've lived 10, 20, 30, or more years in another country without learning to interact comfortably!

A reply is sent to the discouraged foreigner by none other than the "invisible hand." There is a force, said

Newcomb, that makes a person want to instigate communication, a force that attracts one person to another, a force that makes a person believe strongly in an issue, a force that draws the attention of a foreigner to the rewards of symmetry, a force that instigates orientation! Just as there are stories of international recluses, there are beautiful stories of interaction.

> Esta Moreland arrived in the country on Saturday—a quiet, conscientious college coed. She was met by a host family and immediately taken to her new home. By Sunday afternoon she was "finished." She came to our house, and wept in helpless frustration. She didn't know a word of Spanish, and had no idea how to express even the simplest request or the simplest appreciation. Did she want to go home? *Of course not!* "I merely came to cry, to get some Spanish books, to ask some specific questions."
>
> In a week Miss Moreland was enjoying her stay. In three months she had endeared herself to her host family, her neighbors, and acquaintances. She had learned to touch them with her hands, with her smile, with simple Spanish, and most of all with her love. And she achieved symmetry with many!

There have to be invisible hands urging on the Esta Morelands before there can be communicative acts. Theodore Newcomb's model requires that two people get into orientation about something. Symmetry can't occur without the communicative act.

Objects of Communication

When a foreigner and a native resident begin talking, what is the object of their communication? (You will recall that Newcomb labels these objects the Xs in his model.) While there are trillions of things to talk about, I would

venture a guess that the initial objects of communication
are rather limited in number—the foreigner's personal
needs, such as clothes hangers! Or milk. Or where to find
a bathroom. In fact, one might safely generalize by saying
that most of the foreigner's initial attempts at interaction
have to do with self-centered interests.

There are important implications to that statement. If a
self-centered interest is the initiator of communication, it
might be possible that (using the Newcomb model), the
Xs are more important to A than is the B. In other words,
food or fun or a building lot or a signed contract or a ticket
is the thing wanted, and not the relationship with a
person. How often in my visiting in Costa Rican homes I
made a fuss over the food (an X), when my hosts might
have preferred my expressions of appreciation for them as
friends.

Foreigners go abroad with their agendas (of Xs). One is
going to "take the gospel" to people, another to make
money, a third intending to study "culture," a fourth to do
eye surgery. And many times those agendas are given a
type of authentification by a sending agency, and in some
cases, the "call of God."

The native residents have their agendas also, a fact that
sometimes escapes the foreigner. Some get into communication with foreigners because of curiosity with the
stranger, or because they have a service or a product to
sell, or because there is status in having foreign friends, or
because this foreign friend might give gifts or a
recommendation, or a job, or because there are
dating-mating possibilities, and so on.

There are two agendas. But who wins out in setting the
agenda, the foreigner or the local resident? For some
reason, I seem to recall that etiquette would allow the

host to "be in charge." That seems reasonable, and I would suppose that when foreigners visit us in the United States, most of them let us set the agenda. On the other hand, I carry a suspicion that when we North Americans become foreigners, we insist on setting the agenda overseas. There is power and priority in being a North American, or so we think. This is one reason the weakening of the dollar has been such a psychological blow to us.

Not only do many North American foreigners set the agenda, but they also mix up the Xs as though all objects of communication had equal importance. And all Xs do not have equal importance. There are primary issues, the most fundamental, rooted deeply in the tradition and psyche of a people. There are secondary issues of less importance, yet honored enough to withstand easy exchange. Tertiary issues are those we truck in, the odds and ends of everyday decision-making such as which clothes to wear, which TV channel to watch.

Consider a well-meaning North American meeting a lottery ticket seller on his first trip abroad. The North American gives greetings to the seller, strikes up a conversation about the tropical rain, and then offers his opinion to the seller that the lottery is a financial scandal that discriminates against the poor. The North American mixes a tertiary issue (the rain) with a more important issue (the long tradition of financing the children's hospital through "chances"). When a native resident chats with another resident, both are fairly cognizant of whether the topic of conversation is a primary, secondary, or tertiary issue. But a foreigner, especially an aggressive one, may be a bull in the china shop, crashing into primary issues. A team of foreign medics enter a village for a week, giving out antiparasite pills, inoculating residents against tetanus, spraying houses against malaria, all the while being unaware of that town's internal medical structures. A missionary "converts" the mother of a family, setting off a series of spiritual, social, psychological, domestic changes far more profound than either of them realizes. Fruit companies change the terrain, cutting down jungles and installing straight lines of banana trees—an act that affronts the gods of nature.

I would think it temperate for a North American foreigner to allow the native residents "equal time" in setting the agenda, and to begin communicative acts over Xs of tertiary importance, building up a series of symmetries and confidences before moving into Xs of secondary importance. Concerning the Xs of primary importance, I can only quote a wise missionary: "I just live here and love the people. I let God do the converting."

Some Thoughts of a Religious Nature

I have told orientees in training for overseas work that Christians have no advantage over non-Christians in cultural adjustments. Nor do they achieve symmetry in cross-cultural communication more quickly than non-Christians. I have to believe that, after seeing so many maladjusted missionaries overseas. Among the students I have worked with, the professed Christians have not been better intercultural ambassadors than professed skeptics or atheists. One might even build a case that any person armed with a religious call may have the disadvantage of moral rigidities and social inflexibilities. And more than one person has charged that Western Christianity suffers from cultural intransigence.

What irony in these charges, because Jesus Himself is

universal. Where could we find a better example of a Person, foreigner though He was, interacting with the native residents? He worked for more than mere symmetry. While on earth, He remained in a rather small geographical area, but when others detoured around the undesirable cultures like Samaria, God incarnate deliberately passed through the Samarias, asking the native people for water and giving them the living water. (Study that account in light of the AtoBreX model.) Christ's sacrificial death made a reunion with God a new possibility for all people. "There is no question here of Greek and Jew, circumcised and uncircumcised, barbarian, Scythian, slave and freeman; but Christ is all, and is in all."

To be at one with God gives each man and woman on earth the grace to be reconciled with the neighbor. No wonder professed Christians carry with them a special courage when entering foreign cultures! What Christians forget is that God is the Reconciler, and that He has to move us just as far as He must move the other person in effecting that reconciliation. We are often unwilling to be moved, even by the grace of God.

It would be well for Christian people to study once again the story of Peter's cultural sensitization. "It is not for you to call profane what God counts clean," he was told in his dream. In the reconciliation between Cornelius and Peter, the good Christian Peter was the one who had to travel the furthest.

There are intercultural implications in Christ's mission to earth. The Apostle Paul wrote:

His purpose in dying for all was that men, while still in life, should cease to live for themselves, and should live for him.

. . . From first to last this has been the work of God. He has reconciled us men to himself through Christ, and he has enlisted us in this service of reconciliation.

I find a strong resemblance in the message of the cross and the Newcomb model of communication. While I do not wish to demythologize Christ's work, nor to divinize Newcomb's work, I would nonetheless label as "miracle" that wondrous moment when two participants in communication achieve common union. Call it symmetry. Call it reconciliation. Call it shalom.

Christ, the Reconciler, gives new meaning to the concept of the "invisible hand," for He is often our source of *grace* to love (the Bs) and to be loved (by the Bs) and our source of *conviction* to believe in the good and to eschew the evil (the Xs). Even when we, like Jonah, care little about the people of Ninevah and lack conviction about the message for those people, the "invisible hand" can work wonders!

From the Other's Point of View

"Would to God the gift to give us, to see ourselves as others see us." Especially when the others are people from a culture other than our own.

We might grant ourselves that wish—at least in part—by taking a little self-examination exercise. Ten parts to the exercise, no more.

1. List some of the persons of another culture with whom you maintain a continuing interaction, and with whom you achieve symmetry on many occasions. Do you wish you had more friends of other cultures? Fewer friends?

2. List some of the persons of other cultures who are accessible to you, but with whom you do not maintain interaction. Why not?

3. With whom (of another culture) are you forced by circumstances to communicate? Do you interact about things beyond the minimal requirements of the circumstance? Do you achieve symmetry?

4. Name a person (of another culture) with whom you interact, but usually without agreeing with each other.

5. Who (of another culture) is trying, without much success, to attract your interest? Whom are you trying to attract?

6. Recall an occasion when you tried to reach an agreement with a person of another culture, but the attempt only backfired.

7. Can you remember having brought a person of another culture to agreement with you on something? Can you remember having been convinced to change your mind by a person of another culture?

8. Identify a person of another culture with whom you'd probably agree more frequently if it weren't for a third party that interferes somewhat.

9. Make a list of ten tertiary issues you've talked about with persons of other cultures. Ten secondary issues. Five primary issues.

10. On a scale of 1 to 10, evaluate your cross-cultural communication activities.

disassociation with people of other cultures	interactions with success and failures	achievement of symmetry with others

1	2	3	4	5	6	7	8	9	10

Bananas

*The story of banana production, as judged by
the gringo, and then as depicted by Miguel Angel
Asturias in his famous banana republic trilogy*

The banana, I learned at an early age, was one of
nature's most nearly perfect products. Apparently the
most colicky baby could digest bananas easily. And
although a person might be allergic to eggs and milk and a
wide variety of other foods, bananas could be safely
ingested. Not only were bananas healthful; they were the
foundation for banana splits, surely the best of all possible
desserts.

As popular as bananas have been in my lifetime, it's
hard to believe that a hundred years ago bananas were
such a novelty that a special exhibit of bananas became a
hit at the Centenario of Independence in Philadelphia in
1876.

Can anything be said *against* the banana? Why include
a chapter on bananas in a book about two points of view?

With my sincerest apologies to banana lovers, I must
admit that beauty of persons as well as of bananas is in the

eye of the beholder. And the eye of the beholder is conditioned by "more than meets the eye." Yes, there are two—and more—points of view toward bananas and their production. We shall in this chapter present two such views: (1) as North American entrepreneurs would judge things, and (2) as a Nobel prize winner would perceive reality in a series of three novels called the "banana republic trilogy." The chapter will conclude with discussion about both points of view.

Banana Production, as Seen by the North American Entrepreneur

To put a good crispy apple or a sweet peach or a deep red watermelon onto the table takes a lot of careful work. But how much more so for a ripe, yellow, unblemished banana—at only 20¢ a pound. The country storekeeper's concern about bananas is just a small scene from the last act of a long drama that diminishes fruit growing in the North. A banana's critical purchase period is only 48-60 hours long. It is brought to the retailer's shelf for that crucial sale from a warehouse where a middleman has transported it from agents who shipped it across the waters from a port where boats lined up to be loaded with precious green cargo that was brought to the wharfs by train from inland plantations where workers cut, sorted, washed, and loaded the stems after a year of difficult plantation husbandry.

Bananas grow in awful places—tropical flatlands where temperatures and humidity compete to outdo each other, where yearly rainfall is likely to range from 150 to 200 inches, where jungles seem to be penetrated only by insects that carry malaria. And strangely, those awful places seem always to be located in countries where governments are unstable, workers are more friendly than industrious, and a year's long labor can be splintered overnight by Caribbean hurricanes.

So much more remarkable then, that one North American company—the United Fruit Company (now called United Brands) could have carried 30,000,000 stems of bananas to the United States in 1952 (per capita consumption that year was 17 pounds!),[1] or could have delivered 93,000,000 boxes of bananas to the States in 1975.[2]

Since bananas and the United Fruit Company seem almost synonymous, let us review the story of United Fruit, which may be divided into several eras: 1870-1900; 1900-1930; 1930-1955; and 1955 to the present.

The era of 1870-1900. Down in Costa Rica in the 1870s, 4,000 workers were dying in the process of building the first 24 miles[3] of a railroad through terrain "so rugged that even cart roads were only partially completed."[4] The railroad builder needed something to haul on his railroad, so he planted bananas. Meanwhile, a Boston shipper was learning that he could buy green bananas in Jamaica, transport them to Boston, and sell them at 10 to 15 times the purchase price.[5] He hired a salesman to introduce this new fruit to the eastern seaboard. There was success. By 1899, the railroad builder (Minor Keith), the shipper (Lorenzo Dow Baker), and the salesman (Andrew Preston), formed the United Fruit Company. Its first public offer to stock garnered only $1.65 million, but by the end of one year, the capitalization stood at $11,230,000.[6]

In that first year, United Fruit carried about 16 million stems of bananas out of Central America.[7] But to say that banana planting brought instant success is not accurate.

The work and the risks were incredible. To clear jungles with the *machete,* to dig drainage ditches by hand, to pile up roadbeds and lay railroads, to import railroad equipment and drag the materials by rank of oxen, to build wharfs and find ships—who can exaggerate the headaches? Of Limon, where United Fruit first established itself in Costa Rica, a local highlander's saying was, "He who goes there once is a hero. He who goes twice is crazy."[8]

Few people lived there. Minor Keith tried to coax highlanders to work on his enterprises, but relatively few responded, and those who did were immediately vulnerable to yellow fever, malaria, and other illnesses. He carried 700 convicts and rabble from New Orleans, but only 25 survived.[9] Later he brought hundreds, thousands, of Jamaicans and Chinese to the front lines of his economic battle. Many died, including three of Keith's brothers, but Keith and United Fruit won. By 1908, Keith was planting 34,000 acres to bananas.[10]

The era of 1900-1930. If one labels the era from 1870 to 1900 the foundation years of struggle, then one may justifiably call the next 30 years glorious victory for United Fruit Company. Profits in 1920 alone totaled $44.6 million.[11] Wrote a company employee:

> We had our own army of workers (at one time 90,000 of them), our own navy in the Great White Fleet, our own air force, our own police. We had enormous economic and political power. We owned more land than the half-dozen smallest countries in the world put together. We controlled natural resources that ranged from timber to mineral reserves and soil so rich that in some regions even thirty feet below the surface the loam was still black with fertility. We raised our own food—not only bananas—but were also one of

the largest cattle farmers in Central America. And because we were so nearly self-contained we were almost invincible.[12]

By 1930 the company was shipping 65,000,000 stems of bananas yearly on its Great White Fleet of more than 100 ships.[13] The company's capital had risen to $215,000,000.[14]

The era of 1930-1955. United Fruit then suffered through, but survived, the Great Depression. Profits in 1932 fell to a mere $6,200,000.[15] But worse than the Depression was Panama disease whose only cure seemed to be in letting the land lie fallow but flooded for two or three years. In Costa Rica, for example, United Fruit was forced in the 1930s to abandon its vast plantations around Limon, and move *en masse* to the Pacific coast. Another disease, Sigatoka, required the spraying of "Bordeaux mixture" over 5,000 infected acres at a cost of half a million dollars.[16]

Survived, yes. By 1952, the United Fruit Company owned or controlled three million acres, engaged in more than a third of the international commerce in bananas, and from its 300 company stores alone gained $3 million in profits.[17] By 1955 the balance sheets showed assets of $390 million, of which $98 million was liquid—cash in the bank.[18] There were 72,860 holders of 8,775,000 shares of stock, each of which gained a $3.00 dividend.[19]

The era of 1955-1977. In recent years the company has taken a wild roller coaster ride. In the first three years of this period, disease destroyed 3,500 acres of fruit. More than 5,000 workers had manned the extensive plantation of Quepos, Costa Rica, in 1947. By 1956 only 700 to 800 were needed, because the company was forced to give up bananas and instead cultivate African palms for oil.[20] But the paper value of the company continued rising. In 1965 one could buy a share for $17. In mid-1968 shares were selling for $60. Stock was selling at 13 times earnings.

Then the 1970s brought on "a case study in corporate calamity."[21] Caught in the rush of corporations to diversify, the company took on unimportant companies. Then came a raid on United Fruit itself by the AMK Corporation (Morrel Meat) headed by Eli Black who first bought 733,000 shares at $41,000,000 and then added more shares till he had controlling stock. It was later discovered that he paid for this stock with money borrowed against the assets of the company.[22] "Things went from good to very bad." Hurricane Fifi destroyed much of the Honduras crop. Stock that was worth $60 in 1968 had fallen to $3 a share in 1973. The company suffered a $71.3 million loss in 1974.[23] The suicide of Mr. Black, the chief executive, preceded news of company payoffs to a Honduran official and set off bitter strife in the board rooms. In a meeting called to consider a successor to Eli Black, one director tore the telephone from the wall so that another director, cruising the Carribean, couldn't call in his vote. [24]

The company has reportedly regained its equilibrium. Stock moved up to $8 by 1976 and hovers between $8 and $9 today. But company losses have not only wiped out the $100,000 of liquid assets but have put the company into arrears requiring loans so large that interest alone is taking $25 to $30 million annually. Dividends have not been declared on common stock for several years nor on preferred stock for even more years. On the other hand, the company has established better relationships with producer countries which in the future could insure more stable interactions than anytime in its history.[25]

From the point of view of North American consumers and stockholders, the company has not been without virtue. Central American governments have been only too glad to let a company such as United Fruit penetrate its virgin jungles and there try to develop resources. That development has meant for most of the banana republics new ports and transportation facilities, migrations of people, and more services. Further, these same countries who are always strapped with an imbalance of payments find a source of revenue from banana exports. In Costa Rica for example, coffee and bananas made up 80 to 90 percent of the exports from 1937 to 1954.[26]

As the company assured its own productivity, it yielded many benefits to workers—high salaries (when compared with other national salaries), company stores, schools, clinics, churches, even electrical systems. Here is an account by a visitor to a tropical division in Costa Rica:

> In every tropical division, there is a section known as the pueblo civil, the civil town, most often right alongside the company town which usually is on United Fruit land. The difference between the two is day and night. The company town is painted and manicured with flowers and fences and lights on the corners. The civil town has a trench of open sewage down the main street, with poverty and sad sights everywhere . . . the *cantinas,* or bars, and the whorehouses.[27]

The company has not extracted an exorbitantly high rate of return. According to company figures, the rate of profit from 1928 to 1955 has averaged 11.1 percent. This restraint has assured the American housewife of one of the cheapest fruits available. Bananas sold for 16.4¢ in 1952 and only 16.5¢ in 1973, although there are upward trends now.

United Fruit, furthermore, has turned much land back to Central American countries. Already in 1935 it donated 250,000 acres to Costa Rica which were apportioned to landless farmers. In 1942 the company donated funds and expertise to found the widely respected Panamerican Agriculture School in Zamorano, Honduras. In 1976 the company sold to Honduras 190 miles of railroad track and right-of-way, plus two wharves for $1.00. One might also mention United Fruit's voluntary rewriting of contracts when Central American countries initiated their programs of income taxes.

In summary, United Fruit Company stands as a symbol of business genius that has done the impossible task of making the jungles produce not only bananas but profits for owners who risked the dangers and outwitted the odds. United Fruit stands as a symbol of the business enterprise that prospers in the highs of profits and pleasures, and suffers in the lows of hurricanes, Panama disease, and death. And United Fruit stands for Chiquita bananas, that enliven our breakfasts, add a sparkle of sunlight to lunches, and "make" the famous banana split.

Try to keep this picture of bananas in mind as we turn now to a different point of view. We shall return later to discuss both points of view.

Banana Production, as Seen by a Famous Central American Writer

Asturias, born in Guatemala in 1899, served in the diplomatic corps of his country but was forced into exile for eight years because of his political convictions. The banana republic trilogy by Miguel Angel Asturias includes three novels entitled *Strong Wind,* [28] *The Green Pope,* [29] and *The Eyes of the Interred.* [30] The account that

follows is my own very brief summary of the action in the
three books—action that spans three generations, two
cultures, and a universe of emotion. Citations are listed
by number of book, then page number, as found in the
English translations by Dell Publishing Company.

In the tropical lowlands of a country—obviously located
in Central America—in "a land that swallows people up"
(1-26), men try to wrestle acreage away from the jungle for
a North American banana company named Tropbanana.

> The work gangs passed by one after the other in groups of
> five, ten, with all kinds of tools, as the foremen led them to
> the low-lying places where the silence swallowed them up,
> the silence and the perceptible boiling of minute insect
> species, invisible but latent, orchestral, frantic, while the
> sun rose up over bonfires of motionless vegetation and the
> breath of marshes, the burning coal of noon. (1-8,9)

Extraordinarily difficult work. Here a man broken by a
falling stone, there a man hot with malaria, over there a
man swelled from the bite of a rattler. But slowly, slowly,
"hands and mechanical equipment [were modifying] the
terrain." (1-1)

Among the sweating workers is Adelaido Lucero,
recently come from the central highlands. To get double
the pay he might have earned at home? To live an
adventure? Who can say why a young man leaves father
and mother and community for the unknown? One day, in
attempting to help a fallen comrade, Adelaido comes
upon a girl whose flirtations draw him to her. When her
parents think he has lain with her, they force a marriage.
Adelaido seems not to mind. After he builds her a house,
he paints the top part of the walls pink and the base
yellow. She thought it would be ugly like that. And he

agreed that it would indeed be ugly. "That's how you were
dressed, Roselia de León, the day I first set eyes on you."
(1-19)

Don Adelaido is in the tropics to stay, and before long,
we find him foreman of a plantation. Here is banana
harvest time:

> The movements of the cutting crew at the foot of a banana
> tree which looked like a green cross resembled those of Jews
> with ladders and spears as they tried to lift down a green
> Christ who had been changed into a bunch of bananas which
> descended among arms and ropes and was received with
> great care, as if it were a case of an overdelicate being, and
> carried off in small carts to receive its sacramental bath and
> be placed in a bag with special cushions inside. (1-25)

In sharp contrast to the natives are people such as John
Pyle and Carl Rose and John's wife, Leland, and Tury
Duzin—North Americans:

> Workmen, foremen, overseers, even administrators, the
> human organization was arriving, it could be said, because
> from that time on, with a different type of man, the blind,
> implacable machinery was beginning to work, one which
> converted everything into figures in its books, unalterable,
> chronometric, precise. (1-28)

They came because "water, sun, moon, stars all join to
produce the bunch of bananas that will be sold for its
weight in gold." (1-28)

One North American, however, stands in contrast to
the others. Named Cosi, he walks the jungle lands,
"half-barefoot, with hand-me-down clothes, no hat, crazy
. . ." (1-39) selling "everything a seamstress needs." His
words are accompanied by a laugh, "Ya-ha, ha, ha, ha!" that

"bubbled up out of his mouth like gargled water that had burned him as he swallowed it and which he then spat out." (1-35)

Leland, the beautiful and sensitive wife of executive John Pyle, falls in love with Cosi, leaves her husband, and marries the hut-to-hut huckster.

We have introduced some of the natives. We have talked about some of the foreigners. There is yet another group of characters, numerous and ubiquitous and totally consequential. Shall we call them the witch doctors, the high priests of the occult, the hoary-headed divines and prophets, the graveyard visitors, the mysterious mermaids of the sea? We are introduced to them by Asturias when he tells how the Shaman Rito Perraj cured a woman of hysterics:

> He had them hoist her up a coconut tree with her legs open as she rose, giving the impression that she was not being raised by the ropes around her shoulders, but that she was climbing by herself using her hands and feet, as she rubbed up against it, massaging herself, feeling herself. It worked. The good lady went for a year without any more attacks. (1-49)

Neither logic nor systematic observation nor statistics nor rational analysis can begin to contain these spirit people; consequently they remain nothing more than weirdos to Anglo-Saxon readers. And just so, the people associated with Tropbanana never intercept any important messages from them. Tropbanana is the loser, of course, because the spirit people deal with the mysteries of life and death and identify with the inexplicable natural elements.

Gringos, in contrast, are demythologized and live in a

demythologized place— "lands where there was no land, where everything was made of steel, glass, concrete, and even the people were like canned goods. Hands without mystery, scrubbed and disinfected, would lift the tropical fruit to their mouths with teeth that had been brushed with foaming toothpaste, and from the mouths down through throats without tonsils to the stomachs·of animals who were almost vegetables." (3-414)

We now know the groups of characters who people the banana republic trilogy. In book 1, entitled *Strong Wind*, the action is propelled by Cosi (or Lester Mead). Cosi to the natives, Lester Mead to the company people. One local Indian leader, in a burst of anger against the North Americans, said, "They're all a . . ." but cut himself off. "I almost said something dirty and Don Lester is and at the same time isn't from their country." (1-96)

In all matters, Cosi sided with the local people. When the Tropbanana decides to drastically cut the price paid to local land owners for their crops, Lester argues with the general manager and urges the local people to withhold their harvest because "making deals with injustice is the beginning of the whole moral defeat of our so-called Christian civilization." (1-97)

The poor huckster even travels to Chicago, Tropbanana's headquarters, and there, before the top man, who was "stuffed into a gray suit of very fine material, a salmon-colored shirt of Italian silk, a yellow tie" (1-100) pleads for his people:

> If the stockholders only knew what it is like to cultivate a piece of land, plant banana trees on it, and when the first fruit appears like the sweetest hope in life, to take it off to be sold, carrying it with great difficulty and care in oxcarts or on muleback and laying it out where it can be bought, and to

wait under the sun for hours on end, filling themselves up
with illusions about the benefits gained from the fruit of
honest work, and suddenly to receive a negative answer
. . . . (1-101 & 102)

The top man, called "The Green Pope" raps his
knuckles on his desk and immediately a man appears from
behind the curtains, cradling a submachine gun, "tiny like
a pet." (1-103) Cosi retreats, but not without a
"Ya-ha-ha-ha-ha! . . ."

Cosi returns south, organizes several local landowners
(including the Luceros and several households by the
name of Ayuc Gaitan), and sells bananas independently.
He once delivers a load of bananas free to a hospital in the
capital. "How wonderful for them to send us these
bunches of bananas," a Sister of Charity comments,
"because all we've been getting from there are the
incurably ill!" (1-117)

Mead stood watching a procession of living corpses.
Human bones that were coughing and spitting blood. Eyes
bulging out of faces soaked in bitter quinine perspiration.
Teeth attempting a tragic laugh between the dry edges of
their lips. The stench of weeping and of diarrhea. The sick
people bundled up their clothing to carry, those who could
walk, the others, on brown canvas stretchers, were carried
inside from the ambulances by barefoot attendants in white
gowns. (1-117 & 118)

"Wealth piles up here in a fantastic way," said one
company man down in the tropical lowland. "The figures
are astronomical. If a child began to count what has been
earned from bananas, not counting peso by peso, but
counting by thousands and thousands of gold pesos, he'd

be an old man before he got to the final figure." (1-137)

Tension between the local people and Tropbanana drives Cosi northward once more where his astonished wife, Leland, learns that her single-hearted husband is really a major stockholder of Tropbanana, but a lone voice crying in the wilderness for justice and peace.

Still no success. And then, no sooner do they return to the tropics than a vicious hurricane slams into Tropbanana. Who can explain the ways of the winds? Ah, the spirit people. An Indian, Hermenegilo Puac, had been wronged by Tropbanana and has cursed, "Gringo sons-of-bitches, if they've got something that can't be seen and crushes us and which a person can't fight against, not even by killing, we too, ha! I'll [mutilate myself] if there isn't some kind of revenge!" (1-211 & 212) He goes to the shaman and asks for an invincible force that would ruin all the *gringos*. The shaman asks for his head, and Hermenegilo Puac gives him everything as long as there would be vengeance.

A pact had been made; the shaman kept his word. He digs up Hermenegilo's head from the grave, dips it in lime water, and waving it, calls for the winds. The winds come.

> The presidents of the company, the vice-presidents, the local agents, the superintendents, the . . . all of them, all the representatives of the great people up there, those people who had neither face nor body, but did have an implacable will . . . . All of them were spinning about like blond rats, dressed in white, with eyeglasses on their poor myopic eyes, in their tumbling houses that were about to be torn up and swept away. (1-213)

Even Cosi and Leland.
End of book one.

George Maker Thompson, a burly undaunted ship-
owner who plied the ports of Central America, is installed
as general manager of Tropbanana. He is determined,
brash, and brutal. When a beautiful young girl, Mayari,
hears of his calculations to disenfranchise poor landhold-
ers, she tries to tempt him away, but fails. She dresses in
her white wedding gown and jumps into the river.

Thompson hardly needs time for recovery. He marries
the girl's hardened mother, Florona, and proceeds to
clean out the settlements of people and to take their land.
In childbirth, Florona dies, but her child, Aurelia,
survives.

> On the desk of the Green Pope, the supreme commander
> of the plantations, the master of checkbook and machete, the
> great navigator in human sweat, three portraits sat in a row:
> that of Mayari, killed in action, as he used to say to himself,
> remembering her impetuousness before she jumped into
> the river, setting off. . . in search of the signatures of [local
> people] against the expropriations; that of doña Flora, with
> whom he contracted matrimony, also killed in action, he
> used to say ironically, for having died while giving birth to
> the girl who occupied the third silver frame on his desk,
> Aurelia Maker Thompson. (2-102)

How can one adequately depict this twentieth-century
conquistador? Perhaps by showing one event. When a
stockholder from up North pays a visit, and asks tough
conscience questions about growing bananas, Thompson
maneuvers a train accident that kills off the detractor.
About the only person he doesn't control is his daughter
who, when she returns from boarding school, gets
pregnant in a *rendezvous* with an archeologist.

Thompson climbs. His power leads to dreams. In
Chicago he urges Tropbanana to lead a move to annex

onto the United States the lands now controlled by Tropbanana. He is so popular and powerful that his name is proposed for the presidency of the company, but then he learns that he was totally mistaken in identifying the stockholder he thought he had killed in the train accident. It was a man by the name of Peifer. He thought he had exterminated a competitor Richard Wotton, but now learns that Richard Wotton had sneaked into the Tropbanana plantations as an archeologist.

Back in the banana republic, the native peoples learn that Lester Mead and his wife, Leland, not only had been major stockholders of Tropbanana, but that they had prepared wills, leaving all of their $13,000,000 worth of shares of stock to seven local families—including the Luceros and the Ayuc Gaitans.

The local peoples are thrown into shock by these events. First by the mystery of it all.

> Did Lester and Leland sense their approaching death? Had they spoken about dying as they did, holding each other in the midst of the terrible hurricane? Was it true that a gypsy woman had predicted that they would die like that, victims of a strong wind, which [Mead] had interpreted as meaning that the workers would rise up against them, and had therefore hastened to counteract the evil omen by establishing the . . . [company with Lucero and Ayuc Gaitan families]? (2-176)

And the shock is caused by the money. What shall the new heirs do with it all? There is a fear of money that we North Americans can hardly appreciate. Said one lady, Señora Gaudelia, "The best picture of the devil is money. It's the devil himself, with tail, horns, and everything . . . ." (2-277, 278)

George Maker Thompson cannot abide the thought
that some local people control a big block of stock. He
argues with the vice-president of Tropbanana about it.

> A straight line in matters like this, and I think I've had
> more experience than the vice-president, does not get good
> results in Central America. I don't know, but it may be
> because of the geography, the countryside, because in
> Central America, as you must have noticed, a curved line
> dominates everything, and people who follow a straight line
> fail. The adaptation of our rectilinear mentality, our vertical
> conduct, our plumb line business has doubtlessly been one
> of the triumphs of our company. In Central America,
> physically and morally, one has to follow a curved line,
> looking for the line of convenience, whether it's a question of
> building a road or seducing an official. And in this case, since
> there has already been a misunderstanding among the heirs,
> we must take advantage of it, giving our support to those on
> our side." (2-252)

Thompson masterminds a border dispute, and charges
that the dispute is being initiated by a powerful banana
company in the neighboring nation, a company called
Honey Fruit. With the help of government and
journalistic cronies, Thompson makes it look certain that
Tropbanana will fall. Its stock drops drastically. Most of
the heirs sell off their stock at great losses. George Maker
Thompson is the buyer, of course. But what will move
Lino Lucero? Wining and dining? A promise of political
power? Clandestine messages? Threats? A beautiful
woman? Lucero never sells, but Thompson wrests from
him his vote in the upcoming company's presidential
elections.

Book two focuses largely on the Green Pope. Book
three takes us to another extreme—to the situations that

foster guerrilla warfare, and to the warrior of the people, Tabio San. The book opens in the capital city where *gringo* marines are swilling at night in a bar, drunken beasts who destroy property and humiliate servants. One such servant is Anastasia, a mulatto whose brother Juambo had been George Maker Thompson's servant who now guards his mansion in the capital. Another sorry broken servant is Nepo Rojas, old and frail, who rides his bicycle home after the brutal nights at the bar. One day while sleeping in his hut, someone breaks in and pleads for protection.

This someone is Tabio San. He has been an outlaw since the day he felt sorry for birds that were captured and sold. He assaulted the captor, a Sr. Roncoy Dominguez, and then opened all the birdcages. Gradually he became more and more alienated from society and according to the government indictment was an arms smuggler, a drug pusher, and a white-slaver. He had been hunted in every crevice of the highlands for having assisted in an attempt on the life of the president.

But the government indictment is not the window through which we see Tabio San. Asturias shows him as the hunted one, as a human being in love with a schoolteacher in an isolated mountain village, as a free spirit opposed to any kind of chain, as an altruistic fighter for whom the principle of liberty is far more valuable than his life.

His movements, like all of the other principle characters of the banana republic, are guided not by the dollar, but by the spirits. His guide is not the shaman of the Pacific lowlands (although he could have understood the voice of the shaman) but by a cart driver, Cayetano Duende, and a mountain potter, Popoluca.

In the capital, Tabio San disguises himself as an ashman—a person who goes door-to-door to clean the stoves in the huts. His name is legendary, and in his new role he spreads the gospel of revolution. Among his converts—Juambo, the mulatto, who decides to return to the lowlands, and there to do penance for the years of serving the Green Pope, by carrying fruit upon his back like his own father did.

We follow Juambo back to the region where Cosi and Leland had once lived. Back to where Lino Lucero now lives not in a cottage painted pink and yellow, but a house guarded by soldiers, "which isn't a house anymore but a palace out of the *Arabian Nights*." (3-379) Back to a place now rife with revolution where the military is camped against the townspeople, where mayor is at odds with main merchant, where local priest is forced out under military orders.

There, Juambo does penance and pays a debt to his father:

> Juambo crushed an ear. That first day of his great payment . . . . The ear beside his decayed molar. But he kept on carrying, without letting himself be squashed by the hostile bunch, beyond the limit of his creaking bones and his bloodshot eyes and, unlike his comrades, without drawing from the greenness of his load the hope of freeing himself someday, their hope of fleeing that hell and going back to their villages.
> Yes, his comrades embraced their hope as they lifted up the bunches and threw them onto their backs, their heads down so that the rough blow would land on their shoulder blades, which they covered with horse blankets, and some had baskets which they made into cones to cover their heads.
> Juambo was embracing his punishment with the desperation of a person who knows that he has no salvation, with teeth,

sweat, tears biting him. He was perspiring, his tears flowed
and he bit his lips from the pain in his ear. It got squashed by
itself and it would have to heal by itself. It would have to
unsquash itself since it had squashed itself. It hurt up to his
hairline. (3-341)

And what had become of the native peoples Juambo
had earlier known?

Yes, there aren't many of us left. Everybody knows that on
the coast people don't last long, and even less the people who
were dispossessed. My father died, the Marins and the ·
Salcedos died . . . . (3-88)

Yes . . . our people disappear. The victims and witnesses
of their cruel methods are easy food for death, and since
there's no memory between fathers and sons here, they can
wipe out a whole generation and then with the same
impunity they wipe out another and another." (3-89)

. . . Stealing our land, changing people who had a good
living into a bunch of beggars, and, no power! What hurts
most is no power, not being able to do anything against
them. . . . Only someone like me, who's been through it
with his own flesh knows what it's like!" (3-89)

Cosi's money, unfortunately, accomplished little.

What's come of all that money? . . . A bunch of kids who
talk English, who dress like gringos, who live like gringos,
some married to gringo women, people who don't feel that
they come from here even though they were born here . . . .
Can you think of anything worse, not coming from where you
were born? . . . Not a single one of those people who stuffed
their mouths with the foreigner's money . . . understands or
ever will understand what a great thing he did. . . . The
foreigner showed what can be done against the banana
company that started out by grabbing land away from its
owners. . . . (3-43 & 44)

And what shall we say of George Maker Thompson, "the Green Pope, who doesn't have the dove of the Holy Spirit as his symbol, but the eagle?" (3-379) He is in Chicago, dying of cancer.

The place that Juambo finds on the coast is the direct result of Tropbanana's policies, the iniquity of a person passed on to the third and fourth generation, a scene ripe for Tabio San's kind of people-revolt. George Maker Thompson's grandson Bobby is there, but what can be said of him? Let him speak for himself:

> Did you ever notice in the movies how the bodies of people who've been machine-gunned seem to hang on the smoke? That's what should be done to the strikers . . . tecky, tecky, tecky, tecky, hang them on the smoke of the machine-guns . . . tecky, tecky, tecky, tecky . . . like in the movies . . . tecky, tecky, tecky, tecky . . . . (3-534)

Events transpire. Who turns the pages of history? The mysterious powers of nature? The mandates of a curse? The devilishness of man's evildoings? The shrewd organization of a Tabio San? The pages get turned. Bobby, sneaking up to the cottage of a rotten whore, is shot dead. The strike of banana workers is called and is effective — the president of the republic, called "The Beast," is forced to resign. The Green Pope dies. And Juambo runs frightened through the plantations.

Discussion of the Two Points of View

Whatever we may offer as "discussion" turns out, one may suggest, as just another point of view — the author's. Be that as it may, the "discussion" will bring together personal observations and comments from a wide variety of sources.

To begin, let us list a number of words that characterize each of the two points of view presented:

View A	*View B*
— from the North	—from the South
— domination of the jungle	—destruction of land
— putting land to work	—taking land from us
— production-oriented	—people-oriented
— hard-headed business decisions	—impromptu emotional impulses
— individualistic	—communal
— rational	—affective (emotional)
— scientific	—superstitious
— profits or losses	—money or no money, bread or no bread
— mechanistic	
— efficiency	—human
— boldness	—endurance
— money	—fear
— free-enterprise capitalism	—alcohol, women, games —socialism, communism
— collusion with government officials	—plottings with fellow workers
— tragedy-hurricanes, Panama disease	—tragedy: a friend's death

What shall we make of the two lists? Certainly they present a profile of potential misunderstandings that leads almost inevitably to distrust and even antagonisms. My own first encounter with outright hostility occurred in rural Honduras where the little Mennonite church building was occasionally pelted with stones by people who had lost employment when the United Fruit Company some years earlier had pulled its operations out of that community, leaving a generation of people unemployed and unemployable. In stoning the church, the Hondurans did not distinguish between the missionaries and the Fruit Company.

One day in San Jose, Costa Rica, I asked the public relations manager of United Brands for books or films that might show us the positive side of United Fruit's history. He admitted not knowing of any such thing! There is a chasm of hatred represented on one side by the self-congratulatory history of United Fruit, written by Stacy May and Galo Plaza *(La United Fruit Company en America Latina)* [31] and on the other side by a writer such as Carlos Luis Fallas, one of Costa Rica's best-known novelists whose *Mamita Yunai* [32] presents an angry caricature of "Mother United."

Given the perspective of time and distance, what generalities about United Fruit Company and bananas would we offer?

(1) Both Asturias and the United Fruit Company can be accused of presenting less than the whole truth. While Asturias "stacked the cards" against his Tropbanana Company, the United Fruit Company has systematically tried to cover up its own internal operations and to manipulate United States public opinion by a high-class but unprincipled public relations operation.

Asturias, according to Emir Rodriquez Monegal who is editor of *The Borzoi Anthology of Latin American Literature* [33] "embodied, almost too perfectly perhaps, a certain model of what a Latin American writer ought to be: one deeply rooted in his native soil, committed to the anti-imperialist cause, high-sounding and even prophetic in his style." Rodriquez Monegal suggests, however, that the trilogy moves over into "anti-imperialistic propaganda."

On the other side, Thomas McCann, former public

relations director of United Fruit, penned a most revealing confessional:

> I had . . . to take a long, hard look at my own job . . . I looked around my office one morning and took inventory. The first thing I examined was my file of press releases for all occasions. . . . If anything went wrong, I had a press release. . . .
>
> I thought about the real consequences of how I had spent my sixteen years with the Fruit Company. . . . It was a depressing exercise. . . .
>
> The more I thought about it . . . the more certain I became that public relations was helping to screw up the world. In back of almost every bad situation, every lie, every injustice, I could see the hand of the PR man pulling the strings, making things happen, covering things up. . . .[34]

McCann cites case after case of duplicity—even the advertising campaign that tried to nurture impulse buying of bananas by depicting them in ads as eight-inch phallic symbols.[35]

(2) Asturias' Tropbanana illustrates, nonetheless, some of the failures of multinational companies like United Fruit. Asturias depicted the Green Pope (the head field man) as a cold, calculating brute, and the headquarters back home as even less humane. Current economists and critics seem to agree for the most part. Harvard Economist J. Kenneth Galbraith is openly scornful of the company's administration—"an aristocratic business instrument of proper Bostonians which for several generations recruited executives on the basis of family connections and social excellence, and thus got people who were personally elegant but administratively incompetent." [36]

A high-ranking employee from inside the company

wrote, "The management of the United Fruit Company had been content, for the most part, to sit in Boston and count the money and watch bananas grow with the same detachment with which an actuary watches the growth and death of populations." [37]

Galbraith joined other critics in expressing an equally low esteem for United's field managers: "The actual operations in the banana republics . . . [have been] in the hands of hard-bitten independent plantation satraps." [38]

When United Fruit made its dramatic plunge from a profit of $31,000,000 and value per share of $55.00 in 1969 to a loss of $71,000,000 and value per share of $3.00 in 1974, the vultures flying over the carcass told of conservative management that didn't know how to diversify, nor how to deal with the man, Eli Black, who had raided the company. "Poor management" is a label attached to United Fruit, but one must realize that such criticism comes after the fall.

(3) United Fruit, called by one writer "the preeminent symbol of American economic imperialism," [39] followed a philosophy of development that today is rejected thoroughly outside the capitalistic world, and frequently inside it. In the words of company spokesmen:

> We are certain that the influence of investments flowing from the large industrialized nations which generate capital toward nations less developed should be considered the largest instrument for stimulating the systematic development of the nations with less capital.[40]

What's wrong with the philosophy? Simply, it hasn't worked according to the formula. Writes Jose Miguez Bonino, a leading Latin American theologian,

Latin America suddenly perceived that it had indeed been incorporated into the modern world, but not as an equal partner, called to play a more and more significant role in the leadership of this venture, but rather a mere dependent, destined to permit an always increasing profit for the "patrón."[41]

One can readily see the unequal participation of North and Latin America in the production of bananas by identifying what has happened to a dollar that a North American shopper paid for bananas:[42]

Cost and margin of profit for the retailer	$0.25
Margin of profit for the wholesaler	.06
Cost of maturation, and delivery to retailer	.10
Land transportation in the United States	.08
Margin of profit for the importer	.10
Cost of distribution and sales for importer	.04
Shipping over water	.10
Amount for local production	.27
	$1.00

Since United Fruit controlled shipping, importing, land transportation, and wholesaling, the company itself realized the power of money-on-the-move of 48 percent of that $1.00. And only 27 percent went for production. But even that latter figure conceals the fact that only a portion of the 27 percent stayed in national hands since United Fruit owned the land, stores, railroads, wharfs, and related facilities. The earliest contracts provided that United Fruit would pay no export duty. In 1970 it was paying $.003 per stem (a stem averages about 80 pounds).[43]

In other words, "development," if it meant an infusion of capital that stayed within a country for that country's own independent growth, did not happen.

The criticism of the development model includes yet other facets. Denis Goulet, author of a widely used college textbook on development,[44] wrote,

> For developed and underdeveloped societies alike, basic questions are neither economic, political, nor technological, but moral. What is the good life and what is the good society in a world of mass technology and global interdependence? Is fullness of good compatible with abundance of goods? Is human development something more than a systematic combination of modern bureaucracy, efficient technology, and productive economy?

In my reading and in firsthand observations in Central America, I have found little evidence that United Fruit made a moral investment. That was never its intention.

(4) Latin Americans in recent years have used the terms *exploitation* and *dependence* to sum up the North American and the Latin American roles respectively in social, economic, political, and even religious relationships. The gusto that was required for United Fruit to make a success of things in Central America became the natives' own *disgusto*. In what ways may United Fruit have been exploitative?

It is my impression that a chauvinistic style of operation was as damaging as specific acts of intentional dehumanization. One critic has equated the United Fruit Company with a mixture of "John Wayne movie clichés . . . gin and tonics and Dewar's White Label Scotch on tropical verandahs; endless miles of private jungle fiefdoms; natives who were variously brooding, surly or submissive; boots, khaki uniforms, horses and pistols; the Great

White Fleet [the largest private navy in the world]; the early morning produce markets and the colorful, crude men who ran them . . . and behind it all a tradition of enormous wealth and power and privilege. . . . [45]

United Fruit's chauvinism was once described in terms of its policies in hospitality:

> A visitor to a Fruit Company division is either accepted as a guest or he is turned away . . . . Tropical management of United Fruit is famous for its hospitality. If they like you, you're a guest for almost as long as you care to stay, free. If they decide they don't like you, you can't even get on company property. . . . And it was a hospitality that went far beyond free drinks and free food and a free place to sleep: with the right introductions, a guest who expressed an interest in the Mayan ruins, for example, would immediately be loaned the use of a plane and pilot . . . and he would even be given a guide. . . . To visit them was to submit your freedom, your self-sufficiency and your pleasures to the dispositions of a benevolent, all-powerful host. To be employed as a worker was to submit your life and your entire future. And once you had submitted, no country or ideology or system of government on earth had more power over you. That was the price. [46]

If explicit acts of intentional exploitation are hard to document, cases of dependence are not. The workers, brought by Minor Keith to Costa Rica to build the railroad, were promised employment and a ship home whenever they wished to return to Jamaica or other of the Caribbean isles. Practically all, however, were doomed to remain in this alien land, either because there weren't boats to transport them or because they hadn't enough money to pay the fare. To make their situation worse, they were not accepted as first-class citizens. (In Costa Rica, for example, the Jamaican blacks were not welcomed onto the central plateau until 1948.) Their dependence upon the company was tied into the company store on the one hand, and the lack of alternative employment on the other. When disease caused the Fruit Company to relocate, thousands of immigrants were left to eke out a deplorable existence on the edges of the jungles.

(5) Much of the fear of the Octopus, as United Fruit Company was known throughout Central America, was due to its size. Company executives have tried to deemphasize United's size by saying that the company was not among the large or even upper-middle-sized industrial corporations of the United States, and that even some New York department stores were larger. But when seen from the vantage of Central America, the monster looked large indeed. Imagine Minor Keith leasing a whole railroad for 99 years, and holding 8,000,000 acres of land, in a country the size of West Virginia. Imagine one company controlling 3,000,000 acres on one small isthmus and hiring 60,000 workers. During many years of operation Costa Rica's total budget was not as large as that of the company. In Honduras, the fraction of a cent tax per stem represented the largest single source of revenue for the country during many of the years. Imagine 100 ships. Imagine profits of $44,000,000 in 1920 and $70,000,000 in 1952. Imagine that as late as 1955 the export of bananas made up more than 40 percent of the total export of Costa Rica, Ecuador, Honduras, and Panama. [47] Commented one writer, "General Motors is a midget in its effect on the United States economy as compared with United's effect on Costa Rica." [48]

Size alone gave to any action by United Fruit an

influence greater than one might suspect.

(6) Asturias criticized monopolistic policies in his novels. United Fruit has tried to deny such charges. "Facts" shed some light in the case. From the company's founding until 1929 it bought off more than 20 smaller companies. Up to 1910 United controlled 75 percent of banana sales to the United States, and from 1910 to 1930 60 percent of sales. [49] In 1929 it bought out the strong Cuyamel Fruit Company which had been the brainchild of "Sam the Banana Man" Zemurray for "a distressingly large issue of stock" [50] ($31,500,000).[51] After a brief "retirement," Zemurray joined the executive team of United. United Fruit was finally "taken to court" by the Department of Justice in 1954 and directed to divest itself of certain subsidiary and supporting companies. Such divestitures were accomplished by 1972. Today the company has only about 34 percent of the banana business in the United States and Canada, and 27 percent worldwide.[52]

(7) United Fruit has been politically involved in Central America. But has it been as active as Asturias' Tropbanana Company? Did it actually affect local policies, incite revolutions, and influence elections?

Costa Rica's former minister of *hacienda,* Dr. Federico Vargas, said in a recent lecture in San Jose, that during the history of United Fruit Company, no single president was elected in Central America without the support of United Fruit Company.[53]

The words of Tom Buckley in a *New York Times Book Review* article were even harsher: "Generations of Central American politicians [have been] lifted up and

cast down by the company in the furtherance of its
interests, either acting alone or with the help of the
diplomatic and military power of the United States."[54]

United Fruit answers, "Prejudices toward multinational companies and toward United Fruit in particular
are so strong, one can see what he wants to see, and not
what really is." [55]

In defense of the company, one must recognize the
need for a close relationship with governments when an
organization ventures into the highly risky international
field. One must know about authorizations and con-
straints, rules and procedures, precedents and prospects.

But did United go too far?

It is widely known that the Great White Fleet was quite
cooperative with the United States military in both World
Wars. (Germany torpedoed a United Fruit ship near Limon,
Costa Rica in the early 1940s.)

It is reported that two United Fruit ships were used by the
CIA-sponsored invasion of Cuba. (Castro's father had been a
foreman in the company's sugar works. Castro later seized
company properties worth at least $100 million.)

United Fruit directly and indirectly helped to overthrow
Guatemala's President Jacob Arbenz in 1953. Although
United has denied any part in the revolution, Ydigoras
Fuentes, a later president of Guatemala, admitted to having
been asked to lead the revolution. He had been approached
by a United Fruit Company executive and two CIA agents,
one of them being Howard Hunt of Watergate fame. (The
problem that vexed United Fruit in Guatemala was that
President Arbenz was appropriating "unused lands" for
national land reform, and demanded 178,000 acres of land
United had not been using. United asked for $16,000,000
but Arbenz offered $525,000, based on United Fruit's own
figure used in computing its land taxes.) We will not discuss
the manner of the overthrow, although much of the money •

was funneled through President Anastasio Somoza, dictator of Nicaragua. Armed forces were camped and trained on United Fruit land in Honduras.[56]

In 1974 United Fruit, now labeled United Brands, reacted with similar ire when the banana producing countries took a cue from the oil-producing countries, and decided to form a cartel and charge a new export tax of $1.00 for each 40-pound box of bananas. United Brand's concerted opposition to this tax, which would have cost United Brands $20 million a year, seemed to be interrupted when its president, Eli Black, committed suicide in New York on a Monday morning. The shock of his death was exceeded only by the shock of the news only weeks later that he had offered a bribe of $1 ¼ million to General Oswaldo Lopez Arellano, Honduras' chief of state, to reduce the tax there, and consequently to break the spine of the banana cartel.

Beauty, we noted at the beginning of this chapter, is in the eye of the beholder. We from the North think bananas are beautiful. Some have even called them sexy. It is quite difficult, then, for us to understand why a rural Costa Rican man, who saw my family's packed lunch, said of the big lovely bananas, "Hah, you have hunger killers there!"

Nor can we understand why nearly 4,000 rock-throwing citizens in Coacalco, Mexico, stormed the town hall and forced its mayor to eat 12 pounds of bananas as punishment for shooting a workman.

There is more to a banana than meets the eye.

Liberation Theology

*A dialogue between an advocate of revolution
and a more pietistic North American*

To an outside observer, it may seem that every jot and tittle of life has given cause for the peoples of North America and those of Latin America to misunderstand each other. The objects that both peoples see from the same point of view, the experience they commonly share, the values they mutually esteem are few in number.

For example, consider theology around whose table one might expect to find cordial fellowship. Not so. Within the Christian church the differences over "liberation theology"—a distinctively Latin American contribution to religious thought—may be splitting South from North more profoundly than any previous cultural wedge. Even to write about it may be injurious to the reputation of the writer!

While many Latin Americans, particularly youth, have given the ultimate sacrifice—their lives[1] —to the "mission" of liberation theology, many North American Christians haven't even heard of it. Those who have come in contact with the "concept" seem, to the fired-up liberationist, to have yawned indifferently. In North American theological circles, the response has largely been immediate—categorical rejection of this thing that is "neither theology nor liberating."

I sat one day in a liberation theology course reportedly the most popular course of the semester at the Latin American Biblical Seminary in San Jose, Costa Rica. Students who represented many countries south of the Rio Grande were shaking their heads in amazement. "How is it possible," one asked, "that our Christian brothers and sisters in North America aren't with us?" The professor finally responded, "Can you really expect the wealthy parishioners who attend a beautiful, carpeted, plush church surrounded by a large parking lot for large cars in the well-to-do suburbs of Detroit to know the experience of a struggling group of *peones* at San Sebastian who don't have enough food, clean water, dry housing, health, or security?"

One may fairly say that neither could the people of San Sebastian come close to understanding the everyday experience of people living in the Detroit suburbs. It would be hard for disillusioned, embittered residents of cardboard shacks to imagine that if they themselves were members of that Detroit church, they too would not be interested in liberation theology.

One should also point out, that liberation theology is not by any stretch of statistics a commonly held way of life for the majority of Latin Americans. That church too is divided over the issues. Nonetheless, it is fair to say that liberation theology has dominated the debate of the Latin American Catholic Church from the time of the second Latin American Bishops' Conference (CELAM II) in

Medellin Colombia, in 1968 to the third Conference
(CELAM III) in Puebla, Mexico, early in 1979—where
discussion was greatly influenced by Pope John Paul II. (A
brief summary of the pope's contribution appears later in
this chapter.)

Given the fact, then, that widely different points of
view influence the reactions of people toward liberation
theology, let us try to enlarge our own vision by putting on
someone else's glasses, and looking from that point of
view. We will "stage" a kind of dialogue between—

> Mr. John Smith, 50, white, Anglo-Saxon, Protestant,
> business executive, college educated, resident of the United
> States.

> Señorita Rosa Maria Chavez de la Cruz, student, lower
> middle class, Spanish with some Indian blood, nominally
> Catholic, resident of Nicaragua.

John and Rosa Maria are fictional characters, but we
will imagine that John, on a business trip to Nicaragua,
meets Rosa Maria at a small library in Leon, a university
town, and that they take time to talk with each other. We
will have them speak the words of a wide selection of
knowledgeable people. On occasion we will include a
footnote to identify the source of material or to point the
reader to a further elaboration of the discussion.

Rosa Maria will, of course, be speaking as the
protagonist, arguing on behalf of liberation theology. John
as the listener is sometimes the antagonist, usually a
doubter, and on occasion a forthright opponent of
liberation theology.

We only ask you, John and Rosa Maria, to use
nontechnical language, and to avoid jargon. We know you

both are gracious debaters, so you need not try to outwit each other.

John Smith: You seem all fired up about liberation theology, Rosa Maria. But I doubt whether it really rates in theological circles. My son, a student in a first-class U.S. seminary, said that only one course is offered there on the subject, an elective that only a handful of students, mainly MK's [missionary kids] from South America enroll in.

Rosa Maria Chavez: How liberation theology rates in ivy-covered buildings up North doesn't concern me. What does concern me is that I myself continue fighting for liberation.

John Smith: Fighting? Uh, you better tell me what liberation theology is.

Rosa Maria Chavez: Your request is a strange one. For me, liberation theology is a battle, and the enemy is . . . well, the people that you represent—capitalistic exploiters from the North Atlantic countries, especially the United States. So you see, when the enemy asks me to explain myself, I feel a strange mixture of contempt and affirmation.

John Smith: If you feel contempt, then I'd like to know what causes that contempt. Let's go to the heart of liberation theology. Where does it begin?

Rosa Maria Chavez: It begins in Latin America.[2] If you really want to know where it begins, name off the countries in a roll call, and let them answer.

John Smith: I don't know what you have in mind, but I'll play the game. Argentina.

Rosa Maria Chavez: Thirty-six journalists slain in four years of political violence.[3]

John Smith: Bolivia.

Rosa Maria Chavez: One doctor for every 2,200 people (in U.S. one for every 700); life expectancy 46 years (in the U.S. more than 70 years).[4]

John Smith: Brazil.

Rosa Maria Chavez: Two million children abandoned, and another 14,000,000 children living in such grinding poverty that abandonment might be better for them: that's one third of Brazil's youth.[5]

John Smith: Colombia.

Rosa Maria Chavez: Three of five houses do not have running water or electricity; seven of 10 children suffer from malnutrition.[6]

John Smith: Costa Rica.

Rosa Maria Chavez: Like most other Latin American countries, Costa Rica is deprived of its own resources. "Contract laws" throughout the twentieth century have allowed Compania Bananera de Costa Rica (actually United Brands) to take out bananas without paying (1) regular income tax rates, (2) regular import duties on machinery, or (3) adequate export taxes. [7]

John Smith: Cuba.

Rosa Maria Chavez: Since 1959 when Fidel Castro kicked out the foreign-run gambling and prostitution joints in Havana and expropriated large foreign holdings, distributing land, production, and resources to everyone, the United States, through its C.I.A. has made many attempts to overthrow Castro, invade the country [the Bay of Pigs] and even assassinate this Cuban leader.[8]

John Smith: Chile.

Rosa Maria Chavez: Thanks to the efforts of your C.I.A., Salvador Allende, a legally elected Marxist president, was overthrown; 1,000 persons were assassinated the first days of the coup; some 5,000 were imprisoned in Santiago's national stadium.[9]

John Smith: Dominican Republic.

Rosa Maria Chavez: Twice in this century, your marines invaded this sovereign state. The first time, the United States maintained a military rule for eight years.[10]

John Smith: Ecuador.

Rosa Maria Chavez: In the United States, of 1,000 live births the mortality rate is 17.6. In Ecuador, that rate is 71.5—or four times higher.[11]

John Smith: El Salvador.

Rosa Maria Chavez: Population density per square mile is 196.6 (in Canada—2.3; in U.S. —23.0). A few families hold most of the country's wealth and power. One percent of the people control 40 percent of the arable land. Seventy-eight percent of the people struggle to make a living from 11 percent of the land.[12]

John Smith: Guatemala.

Rosa Maria Chavez: The whole world was shocked when it learned that 24,000 people were killed in the 1976 earthquake.[13] Does the world know that since the 1954 overthrow of its president (through the efforts of your United Fruit Company) Guatemala has lost more people through political assassination than through earthquakes?[14]

John Smith: Haiti.

Rose Maria Chavez: These are among the poorest and least educated people of the world.[15] This clipping from the *Miami*

Herald says, "When drought in the countryside drove thousands of farmers into Port-au-Prince, many lived on five cents a day—one penny for shelter, one penny for water, one penny for bread, and two cents for a double handful of rejects from the vegetable market—the sweepings at the end of the day."[16]

John Smith: Honduras.

Rosa Maria Chavez: For every 21 dollars the typical North American earns, the Honduran earns one dollar. That's $331 a year.[17]

John Smith: Mexico.

Rosa Maria Chavez: Politia Icturia of San Andres says that soldiers came some years ago and took his two sons, two brothers, and two nephews—and they haven't been heard of since. How many people are in prison because of political beliefs? None says the government. One hundred to 200 says Amnesty International.[18] Six hundred says a coalition of three political parties.[19]

John Smith: Nicaragua.

Rosa Maria Chavez: For more than 40 years—that's longer than the age of most Nicaraguans—your government and your business interests have propped up the cruel military dictatorship of the corrupt Somoza family.[20]

John Smith: Panama.

Rosa Maria Chavez: Your own Senator Hayakawa said it so well during the debates over the canal: "Why should we give up the Canal Zone which we stole fair and square?" [21]

John Smith: Paraguay.

Rosa Maria Chavez: The repression against anyone questioning the 24-year iron rule of President Alfredo Stroessner has been so bad that this year Domingo Laino, opposition leader, pleaded with your president to stop sending military aid. Laino was, of course, arrested and slugged upon his return to the country.[22]

John Smith: Peru.

Rosa Maria Chavez: In a land where Indians chew narcotic *coca* leaves to relieve the pains of "cold and hunger and history," 45,000 miners went on strike to protest their $2 to $5 per day salary. The government told strike breakers and police to shoot to kill if they had to.[23]

John Smith: Uruguay.

Rosa Maria Chavez: A mass exodus of residents from the country has left behind those who live in fear of hunger and of political retaliations.[24]

John Smith: Venezuela.

Rosa Maria Chavez: The poor are jammed into shack towns; the rich commute to Miami for shopping and weekend fun.[25]

John Smith: Only a sadist could enjoy so grim a roll call. Rosa Maria, fate seems to have played some nasty tricks on this planet earth. One reads of overpopulation, famines, and earthquakes. I can't imagine what it would be like to survive on 1,500 calories a day. And some countries, like my own, are so richly blessed. What can I say? I do give generously through Church World Service. And contrary to many of my conservative business colleagues, I have supported a liberal foreign aid policy in Congress. Since the Marshall Plan, we have channeled billions of dollars to other countries.

Rosa Maria Chavez: You are, indeed, a Yankee's Yankee. Your responses are precisely what we have come to expect of you. Pity. Charity. Handouts. Yes, in our need we accept those handouts, but how can you believe me when I say, "Keep your charity to yourselves."? And, by the way, your blaming fate is, to use your own language, a "cop-out" exceeded in viciousness only by those who would attribute the inequalities of this earth to the predestination of God.

John Smith: I insist. Fate is involved: the natural development of "things," the disparity in "gifts," the vagaries of history, the chance circumstances that make or break a people. Even Jesus Himself said, "You have the poor among yourselves always."[26]

Rosa Maria Chavez: What a gross misreading of history and of Scripture. But let's not discuss the Bible just yet. Liberation Theology does not begin with the Scriptures. It begins, as I said before, with our condition of impoverishment, oppression, and domination. Thirty years ago—around 1950—something important happened in Latin America. We were given a dream by people like you. A hope was born. We knew that we were in bad shape, a traditional and backward society. You gave us a cure: "Integrate your economy, diversify your production, accelerate your industrialization." "But how?" we asked you. "Follow our example. Accumulate capital. Introduce technology and planning. Offer us an attractive investment climate. Don't let political instability wreck progress. And pronto, your economy will expand *naturally*, and will bless you with all kinds of progress and welfare."[27]

John Smith: Yes, I'm glad you mention this. I know of the "decades of development" and the admirable efforts of the International Development Bank, the Aid for International Development, the International Monetary Fund, Kennedy's Alliance for Progress, the Peace Corps, the contributions of multinational companies . . . .

Rosa Maria Chavez: Spare me, please, will you? Organizations such as those have only contributed to our sadistic roll call of death. Let me show you something. Imagine, if you will, a chart that documents the per capita incomes of countries of the Americas in the early 1950s.

John Smith: Yes, I can picture it. [See chart 1 on page 257.] The United States and Canada would be remarkably ahead.

Rosa Maria Chavez: Correct. The per capita income in the United States was ten times higher than that of Chile, Honduras, and Nicaragua. The discrepancy was even greater with countries such as Haiti, Paraguay, and Peru. And now, Mr. Smith, taking into consideration thirty years of your development programs, what would the chart look like?

John Smith: I couldn't tell you.

Rosa Maria Chavez: It looks about the same. [See Chart 2 on page 258.] Inflation and economic activity have driven the figures higher, but the per capita income of the United States is still ten times higher than Chile, Paraguay, and Peru. Twenty times higher than Bolivia, Granada, and Honduras. And more than 40 times higher than Haiti. If anything, the distance has grown greater. Now tell me, how can that possibly be?

John Smith: I would venture a guess that the decades of development were not successful because (1) you have so many revolutions, (2) corruption—foreign aid money went into private pockets, and (3) increased oil prices wiped out gains. And it is only fair to say that the jump in the U.S. and Canada per capita incomes might simply reflect a more vigorous and systematic effort. We do love to work hard, and we're generally an honest people.

Rosa Maria Chavez: Before you settle in with those explanations, you might also consider the following: your reduction of import quotas when our new products competed with yours,[28] your economic blockades when you were disgruntled with our internal affairs, your military interventions, your operations to disestablish our governments,[29] your use of even missionaries as spy agents, the repressive police forces that you trained, the vetoes and adverse votes at crucial moments from the International Monetary Fund and the International Development Bank.

John Smith: And so what is your explanation?

Rosa Maria Chavez: Years ago a British parliamentarian said, "I wish—in keeping with my doctrine of free exchange—to make England the factory of the world, and Latin America England's granary." [30] That is what you have done. You have invested so that you benefit. You use Argentina for your beef and grain, Brazil for your coffee. Chile for your copper, Central America for your bananas, Cuba for your sugar, Venezuela for your petroleum. When you intervened diplomatically and militarily, it was not on our behalf, but to protect your interests. We were brought into the modern world, not as equal partners, but rather as your slaves.

John Smith: Just a minute. Your explanation is much too simple and obviously prejudiced. It passes the buck. You must admit that your problems are at least in part of your own making—a degree of laziness, hankering toward masochistic heroics, an inclination toward personalism and authoritarianism, a tendency toward irrationality—all of which fight against orderly progress.[31]

Rose Maria Chavez: No, to you I will not admit those *gringo* analyses of us, which you use so cleverly to justify your raping of a region.

John Smith: If you will pardon my saying this, you don't at all conform to the stereotype of the Latin American *señorita*.

Rosa Maria Chavez: Thank you. That is a distinct compliment. Fifteen years ago, I may have been a bashful *señorita*. But something has happened to us youth—a turning point in our experience.[32] We young people suddenly lost our patience. We became angry and took to the streets, fighting for the underdogs. And in the process of action and reflection, something happened to us spiritually. Whether we took to the battle as Latin Americans or as Christians, I can't say, but we experienced a crisis of conscience. We saw that our churches had been allied ideologically with the same national and

The idealization of womanhood—charm from an ambiguous smile; or the reality of being a woman—a life of labor, wrinkled hands, sorrow.

Contrasts

In Latin America as on every other continent, including North America, one can usually find what one is looking for — both beauty and ugliness, grandeur and debauchery, love and hatred, power and weakness.

Some scenes reveal themselves in one way to one person, but in an entirely different way to another person. Or shall we say, the eye of one person sees one thing; the eye of another person sees something else.

Jorge Valenciano, a photographer from San Jose, Costa Rica, has challenged himself to record scenes that embody more than one message. In the selection of his photographs that follow, you will find one message—or two—depending on your point of view.

Above: Vehicles with their horse power, or a man with his beast of burden.

Right: A porcelain figure carries a porcelain cross while porcelain saints give porcelain approval; or a human being carries a cross and who is there to notice?

Far Right: One of the more impressive churches in Barrio; Mexico; or one of the less impressive communities in the barrio.

Above: Industry bringing progress and development; or a factory boding pollution and death.

Left: The cross of Calvary, redemption, and new life in Christ; or a rather hard bed.

Right: The
promise—picturesque,
entertaining, daring, sensual,
sexy; or the
reality—dissipation,
decadence, despair.

Below: The national park, a
place to read, meet friends,
and eat a snack; or the
national park, a place to
work for $4.00 a day.

Bottom Right: An afternoon
nap on a sidewalk in San José,
or an alcoholic with no one to
love and no place to go.

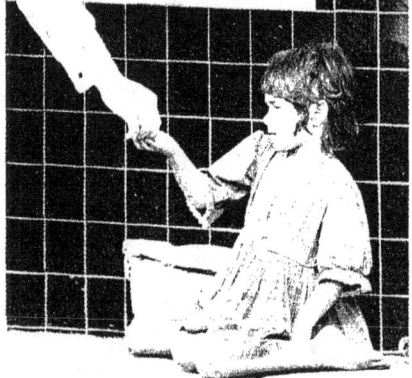

Left: Stationed in her customary place near the tourist store, the little beggar girl looks toward oncoming pedestrians.

Bottom (left to right): (1) Hers is not a world of expensive toys. She has only a bag. She gets her hand ready. (2) A coin. Her eyes fix upon the coin, never noticing the giver nor her cuff-linked shirt. (3) The coin is big. She holds it to her face. Is it a prayer of thanks? (4) She cradles the coin as though it were a doll baby, and looks again. Is it really true?

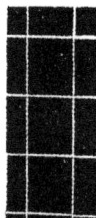

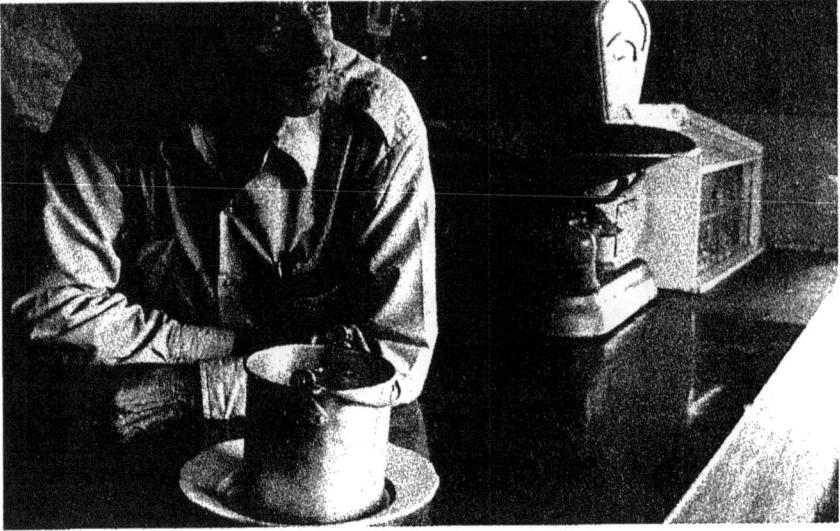

Above: A simple store keeper; or a gaze from emptiness to emptiness.

Right: The legislative assembly building where deputies represent the interests of all citizens; or the street where they park their Mercedeses and Continentals in privately marked and numbered lots.

Far Right: Translated the sign says, "God bless my journey." If He does, the man will sell all his papers and earn $3.00 for the day."

Left: Dogs, the best friends of this child of the slums; or stray mutts spreading rabies, fleas, parasites, and animal feces.

Bottom Left: Rustic, romantic countryside, and simple countryfolk; or isolated rural area, recently robbed of its virgin forests by greedy lumbermen.

Below: The urban area promises a good life, employment, schools, and modern facilities; or marginalized newcomers put up shacks for protection, hoping the city won't come to destroy their shelters.

Above: Laundry and maids; or barbed wire, bucket, scrubbing board, and hot tropical sun.

Left: An outhouse is a joke . . . unless one doesn't even have an outhouse.

Above: Stored in tanks in Limon, internationally financed
petroleum awaits refining; or 80 percent of Limon's housing is
substandard by national norms.

Below: A political slogan sprayed onto the wall calls for
conscience; or a university student, asleep and apathetic.

international forces that for a century left us with little but slavery, malnutrition, illiteracy, forced migrations, unemployment, financial exploitation, and police repression. And we gradually came to perceive that our underdevelopment fed your development. Your multinational companies needed us in this condition to pay a profit to their own stockholders. In our anger, Mr. Smith, we lost some innocence and took up arms.

John Smith: We began with the intention of speaking about theology. Now we're sidetracked on the subject of international warfare.

Rosa Maria Chavez: I'm speaking about theology. I'm speaking of life and death. I'm speaking of an era of death that Spain pressed upon us. And I'm speaking of an era of death that the liberal Anglo-Saxon world is now giving to us.

John Smith: I am confused about this "turning point" that led you into battle. You refer to a crisis of conscience. A change. But this doesn't seem to be the same thing that we call "conversion to Jesus Christ" that leads to salvation and holiness.

Rosa Maria Chavez: You are correct. We are not seeking personal spiritual renewal, nor some mystical and private relationship to Jesus. Our experience has been different, and can be explained only if I use some important Spanish terms. In *committing ourselves* to the cause of liberation from oppression, that is, in *getting into* the action, in *doing* (we call this the "praxis of liberation") we were able to learn a new awareness, to know in a most intimate sense (we call this "concientizacíon") the reality of our profound need.[33] No longer was suffering a theoretical problem, or just a statistical figure, but it was here and now where we were acting. In other words, by *doing* we came to know new meaning. That was our conversion, our crisis of conscience.

John Smith: To me it sounds like politicization, nothing more. Evidently this awareness propelled you to search for answers that are basically nonreligious in nature.

Rosa Maria Chavez: Precisely. Why did decades of development fail? Why have we been kept in dependency over the generations? Why do we have so little when you have far more than you need? We are dealing here with economic, social, and political questions rather than personal, psychological, and philosophical questions, so we have turned to the social sciences for answers.[34] But, mind you carefully, not to the "objective" sociologies you read in your sociology journals.

John Smith: You reject impartial sociology?

Rosa Maria Chavez: Your old sociology has a technical objectivity, a vision of society oriented toward the preservation of the established order. It looks at underdevelopment from a technical point of view, which erases its significance. We knew that we had to revolt against your notions of development. We needed a sociology of change. The answer? Change the sociology.[35]

John Smith: What did you choose?

Rosa Maria Chavez: We had little choice. There were only two options: the economic science of capitalism, or the revolutionary science of Karl Marx. There is no third way, no other alternative. We have opted for Marxism.[36]

John Smith: Wait a minute. Why so categorical? Why only two ways? If there were only two baskets, and we put all of our eggs into only one, we would be really limited. Again, Rosa Maria, why so categorical?

Rosa Maria Chavez: It's interesting to me that you should feel so uncomfortable with two options. That happens, my capitalist friend, to be one more than you allow yourselves. You Yankees have only one option—capitalism. You haven't even given Marxist thought a hearing. Tell me, where in your education were you given a fair introduction to Karl Marx? How many people on your street back in the United States could define the simple *proletariat* and *bourgeoisie* concepts?

John Smith: You largely misunderstand me. I was not referring just to your limiting the choice to capitalism or socialism, but your decision to eliminate the great spiritual resources as an alternative choice. What do you find in materialistic socialism to supply your deepest needs? I should also restate that I, as a born-again Protestant Christian, feel most uncomfortable using Marxism as a way to salvation. Only by Jesus can one be saved.

Rosa Maria Chavez: Let's talk first about Marxism, or socialism, and later about Jesus. Marx has given to us a tool with two sharp edges. On one side, it explains clearly and simply how the social, economic, and political systems of the world work. On the other side, it advocates change, telling us how to transform the world.[37]

John Smith: Okay, I will listen to a lesson on Marxism, if you promise to give me equal time.

Rosa Maria Chavez: First, I will review what Marx "explains" and later I'll mention what he "advocates." The Marxist instrument:

—explains the structures of power in society—who has power and who doesn't have power.
—explains that those with power are few; those without power are many.
—explains that the powerful few become a social class, and the powerless masses become another social class.
—explains that the powerful class gains more and more wealth, and tries to keep that wealth from the powerless class.
—explains that the wealthy class, to preserve its power and wealth, keeps the powerless class in subjection.
—explains that only if the powerless classes are held in a state of continuing dependency upon the wealthy class, can the wealthy class hold on to its power and wealth.
—explains that the wealthy class insists upon the ownership of property, the control of production and of distribution, and operates by the general principles of private enterprise capitalism.

—explains that the ruling class will opt for an oligarchy (the rule of the masses by a few people), but that the government apparatus and political activity and laws will all be forced to serve the economic realm. That is, if the preservation of wealth so demands, laws should be changed.

—explains that this capitalistic class feels quite comfortable with Protestantism with its emphasis on private spiritual piety and a personal morality, in contrast to a religion that would build mainly on a sense of communal well-being.

—explains that the ruling class justifies itself and tries to make its capitalistic exploits look good by using religious symbols such as love, fraternity, liberty, salvation, and unity.

—explains that this ruling class "gives just enough bones to the dog" to keep the dependent classes at bay.

—explains how the powerless masses are forced to be the producers (the workers), but that they can't have what they produce unless they have money (which they don't).

—explains how the powerful try to drive the smaller business person out of operation until a monopoly is formed—all of which results in fewer and fewer wealthy people, and more and more powerless people in the lower class.

—explains why the powerful call this system "natural" and "free."

John Smith: At the moment I am not arguing; I am listening. You suggest that these are descriptions of what Marx saw in the world around him?

Rosa Maria Chavez: Yes, you might call this an analysis of history. If it is a good analysis, it will accurately depict the goings on of life. But Marx, of course, doesn't stop with "explanations." He recognizes that nothing—be it negotiations, compromises, or charity—will cause the rich to give up their powerful position. Therefore, he calls for revolutionary change. More specifically he:

—advocates that property, the means of production and distribution be commonly held.

—advocates that people should work according to their ability

and be rewarded according to their need.
—advocates the organizing of the working classes into a power bloc.
—advocates the forceful overthrow of the capitalists in order to gain power.
—advocates that social well-being rather than personal fortune be given primary attention.
—advocates that people take action now to make real their visions of a utopia on earth.

John Smith: Thanks for your precise summary of Marxism. One thing sticks in my mind, but you didn't mention it. Something about the internal contradictions of capitalism that will cause it to destroy itself in time. That was a Marx prediction, I think. But he's been wrong. I chuckled recently over an article in the widely read journal, *Visión,* about capitalism.[38] The author asked, "Why doesn't it die?" Capitalism is healthy as ever! Since I have equal time, let me talk about my own personal value system.

Rose Maria Chavez: Forgive my arrogance, but I'll state a fact. We know a lot more about your capitalism than you know of our socialism. Your college general education programs are narrow when compared with ours. But go ahead.

John Smith: First, I owe a debt to the Hebrews who helped us understand the God of order. I also owe a debt to the Greeks who taught us the ideals of beauty and truth. And of course the keystone to my philosophy of life is Jesus Christ, who came to bring personal salvation. Now, building on that foundation,

—I revere freedom of conscience, personal faith which the Reformation was all about.
—I believe in natural laws that guide the universe, and that we can harness them through empiricism and the scientific method.
—I believe in free will, in the free use of reason. Man is rational, and with time, comes to truth.
—I appreciate the French Revolution and the American

Revolution, which have given me highly cherished freedoms and personal liberties.

—I believe in social equality, that all people are created equal.

—I believe that the industrial revolution has helped us immensely, and that it has demonstrated that free-enterprise capitalism is a more powerful agent for social well-being and progress than any "imposed" program of the state.

—I am anti-Constantinian. I believe in the separation of church and state. Personal faith and worldly citizenship are two different things.

—And I must say that I'm still optimistic that if we really set our minds to the task, we can use the resources of the world to solve our current problems of nature and man. I see my investments in Nicaragua and in other countries as a personal risk, as a potential for a modest profit, and as a means to put people to work and help them all to progress toward a better life.[39]

Rosa Maria Chavez: Your time's up! If you listened carefully to me, and to yourself, it should be perfectly clear to you that we are engaged in an unresolvable conflict. You speak from the point of view of those "up above"; I speak from the point of view of the "down and outers." Your history is white, Western, and wealthy. My people do not share that history. You are concerned about those who don't have faith; I am concerned about those who don't have humanity. You are calling for personal, individual salvation; I am looking toward social and community liberation. We are in a pitched battle:

— Oppressor vs. oppressed.
— rich world vs. impoverished world.
— developed nations vs. nations held in underdevelopment.
— dominating classes vs. the exploited classes.
— wealthy people vs. those with no money.
— people who eat dessert vs. those who produce the dessert.
— progress vs. survival.

And Mr. Smith, we are about to remake history from the bottom up.[40] We are ready to fight imperialism, oligarchies, and the other sins that bring death upon us.[41] As we commit ourselves to this struggle for liberation, the process of theology takes place. First comes commitment—then comes the theology. And not the other way around.

John Smith: Every time you use the words theology, commitment, and even liberation, I realize more clearly the gap that separates us. The chasm seems awfully wide. When I think of theology . . . .

Rosa Maria Chavez: Nor do I expect you as a member of the rich class to understand or accept this new way. Liberation theology is, yes, a different way of making theology. Your North American theologians begin with an abstract theoretical postulate, and then project it into speculations about life. What are the results? Endless bickerings between your fundamentalists and your liberals. Or worse, a "theology of the death of God" or a "theology of secularization." We turn the process around. First we commit ourselves to making justice for mankind, fighting against the established exploitative system, identifying opportunists and oppressors, and transforming the current historical reality.[42] We pull theology out of its academic ivory tower. Then we discover—in the process of those actions—we discover the presence of the Lord in the heart of the Latin American common people.[43]

John Smith: I think of theology as a conscious discourse about God, His will, and His work in heaven and on earth.

Rosa Maria Chavez: I think of theology as a conscious effort to make possible the life that God intends all people to have. Life in its fullness. Life as shalom. Theology isn't abstract speculation. Theology is action!

John Smith: I'm not convinced that when you speak of "action" you aren't simply adopting a mode of chatter-chatter-chatter, propagandistic and vindictive and political oratory. Prove to me that action is more than this.

Rosa Maria Chavez: Our action includes lots of talk. If you insist on delineating exactly what our commitment means, you'd have to watch those people now in action.[44] For me it means:

—reaching out to the "other" people, taking to myself their suffering.
—releasing those who are in chains.
—helping people obtain the necessities of life: food, clothing, shelter.
—guiding people to realize their full human worth.
—identifying exploitative institutions around us.
—dethroning the false gods of capital and consumerism.
—unmasking the guises that pass as theology and religion.
—reading the texts of the times, to know what's going on.
—getting into politics, to help write current history.
—taking sides in disputes and decisions.
—working toward a utopia that is envisioned by faith.
—transforming the world, effecting change.
—accepting responsibility for myself.
—helping Christians overcome their political paralyses.
—exposing those who use religious symbols for devious purposes.
—integrating salvation and liberation, the sacred and the profane, nature and grace.
—building a new church whose only purpose is to serve the destiny of the poor.
—criticizing current ecclesiastical practice.
—finding analogs in current history that explain the meaning of God.
—rereading Scriptures in light of liberation.
Now don't you think that list reflects genuine action?

John Smith: The list includes a number of admirable Christian service assignments. Many of your items belong on someone else's list—the politician's, the economist's, the social worker's. And I notice that you have finally mentioned the Scriptures. Would you elaborate?

Rosa Maria Chavez: If I had only 25 or 35 isolated verses with which to prove a point, I wouldn't mention the Scriptures. But I don't need to settle on a few verses. I think of my neighbor who said, "All my life I've been reading the Bible. But when I began identifying with poor and oppressed people, all of a sudden I saw things in the Bible that I missed in all those previous readings." Let me just mention several motifs: (1) the salvation/liberation story of the children of Israel from Egypt—involving economics, politics, social relations, exploitation, civil disobedience—everything we've been talking about;[45] (2) the message of the prophets, as they denounce all forms of injustice and oppression;[46] (3) Jesus' announcement of His mission

> The spirit of the Lord is upon me . . .
> to announce good news to the poor,
> to proclaim release for prisoners
> and recovery of sight for the blind;
> to let the broken victims go free,
> to proclaim the year of the Lord's favour.[47]

(4) the Sermon on the Mount which "reverses" so many of the dictates of current wisdom;[48] (5) the ministry of Christ, as He opts every time for the down-and-out person; (6) the resurrection, and the power it gives to believers to carry out Jesus' complete mission, even if it leads to imprisonment and death; (7) the recurring denunciation of the rich and the oppressors, and the recurring benediction on the poor who are oppressed.[49] Even conversion is seen as a change *in action*. Mr. Smith, how is it possible that the directors of repressive regimes can take communion if all of their actions negate the gospel of life? How is it possible to consider as Christians those who are stockholders in big companies, those who demand profits that require production which mortally exploits the workers, those who speak of human rights but at the same time send military aid to dictatorial regimes so that those regimes can clear the way for transnational companies? How is it possible that bishops, archbishops, priests, and pastors continue to give communion to those who are nothing less than the personification of death?[50]

John Smith: I know you feel deeply about the matter, yet you come across to me as a skilled rhetorician and propagandist. Let me think more deliberately and rationally, and I invite you to do so too. Your mention of Scriptures — good. What you have cited from the Scriptures can indeed be found in the Scriptures. We should study these themes more. But Rosa Maria, you have made of Scriptures an ideological textbook. You've turned the Bible into a political tract. You've turned God into a revolutionary, the people of God into a revolutionary army, His purpose into some type of humanization, and the Word of God into revolutionary writings.[51]

Rosa Maria Chavez: Your criticism is direct; we must take it seriously. My response is not meant to be flippant.[52] Look what the Nazis did under the justification of an ideology! Let me approach your question by referring to praxis as obedience. Not obedience to Marxism, but obedience to faith in God. In the Old Testament the Word of God was not a mere transmission of a concept, but rather a creative event that carried out the promise and the justice of God. That Word was not just an ethical guide. It was a call to the children of Israel to follow in obedience, involving themselves in the work of God. To obey meant to do God's will. Later Jesus — who was described as the way, the truth, and the life — talked time and again about faith and obedience. John spoke of doing the truth. Paul referred to faith as a manner of walking. James' epistle is filled with the terminology of doing. We *do* our obedience in a historical context.

John Smith: But why should that "obedience of faith" take on a political coloration?

Rosa Maria Chavez: That's the way theologians are! They reflect, consciously or unconsciously, the societal values around them. One has to ask which type of practical workmanship is reflected by this or that theology? Your theologians have reflected the presuppositions and priorities and point of view of the Western, privatized, dualistic, work-oriented, rational person.[53] Our theologians are reflecting something else. While we are concerned with the scriptural accounts of people carrying out a social, economic, or political act of obedience to faith, your theologians have hardly ever considered that Christ Himself chose actions that had specific political significance . . . and that eventually brought Him to a revolutionist's death.[54]

John Smith: But why should the example of Christ (whom I do NOT think was a political revolutionary) push you into socialism?

Rosa Maria Chavez: Because we can't accept the behavior suggested by a capitalistic interpretation of progress. That interpretation, we think, is exploitative, oppressive, and murderous. That is what leaves in its wake a world of impoverished people. Up to this point, Marx has served much better to give an accurate analysis. . . .

John Smith: Analysis. What do you mean? Give me a specific example of a capitalistic and a socialistic analysis so that I can better see the contrast.

Rosa Maria Chavez: All right. Let's consider "the poor." The capitalistic interpretation goes something like this:

> The poor are a regrettable fact of life. Some people are given one talent, some are given two talents, while others have five. Talent, combined with industry, brings its just rewards. Some people become richer than others. Some people become poorer than others. There is also the factor of fate (or, in religious terms, the smile of God) that brings special blessing to a select few. It is desirable, then, for the rich to be thankful for their blessings and to share in appropriate ways.

That, as I said, is the capitalistic interpretation of "the poor." Now, here is the interpretation according to Marx.

> The poor are not just a fact of fate. Their existence is not politically neutral nor ethically innocent. The poor are a by-product of the system in which we live, for which we are responsible. They are the marginal members of our social and

cultural world. Furthermore, the poor are the oppressed, the exploited, the ones deprived of the fruit of their own labor, those robbed of their own humanity. For this reason, the poverty of the poor isn't just a call for a generous act of charity to alleviate it, but a command to build a distinctively different social order.[55]

So Mr. Smith, only with that different social order can people be free to know the full life in Christ. We must, of course, constantly ask whether the socialist analysis and projection correspond adequately to the facts of human history. So too, you must ask, as you probably never have, whether the analysis of history by which you live gives you an intelligent faith and a strategy for your obedience. How sad that some should be condemned to hear nothing but an echo of their own ideology.[56]

John Smith: Your decision to transform the social order through revolutionary force makes a mockery of the gospel of peace and reconciliation. Love is replaced by hate. Good will is replaced by the fear and horrors of warfare.

Rosa Maria Chavez.[57] If you are trying to recommend pacifism, you'll not receive a hearing from us. The pacifist, by "keeping the peace," is in reality supporting the status quo and thus taking the side of the oppressor's evil system.

If you are trying to advocate a political policy of nonviolence, consider that that policy may, in the end, cost more human suffering and loss of life than a quick, decisive stroke of force. If you are trying to model Christ, study Him again. The rich young man whom Jesus "loved" was told in direct language by Christ to renounce his wealth. Christ criticized the privileged scribes and Pharisees violently and consistently. He reacted with force against those who commercialized the temple area. He called Herod "that fox." And He was considered a political adversary.

Violence is an essential part of the natural growth process, the eruption out of the old and into the new. Violence is an ingredient in creativity. History reveals that no significant human group, no ruling social class, no imperial rule has ever voluntarily, and without pressure, relinquished its power.

Nonresistance is powerless. Violence is necessary to conquer the evil that blocks God's will to reign and man's will to love. Love your enemies, yes. But hate evil with the passion of your faith. There is no room for pacifism or neutrality.

John Smith: No, no. You are wrong. Those who live by the sword shall perish by the sword.[58] I fear that you are facing devastating disillusionment when you discover that you may have selected the wrong political side to fight on. Jesus' kingdom, He said, is not of this world, or else He would call His servants to fight.[59] Rosa Maria, you have been kind enough to inform me of liberation theology. But I find little in it to agree with. In fact, I firmly oppose it. I may be too quick to judge. Let me think through what you said.

Rosa Maria Chavez: Yes, the Anglo-Saxon way. The German way. Think things through. Come up with a new theoretical construct. And meanwhile your 200 million *gringos* will feast on more than $7,000 per capita this year, while 200 million Latin American residents will try to eke out an existence on $75 per capita. While you deliberate hundreds and thousands will die each day . . . .

* * *

The discussion continues between John Smith and Rosa Maria Chavez de la Cruz, but we shall leave them. Not being a fiction writer, I'm not sure how to bring their conversation to a close! Keep in mind, however, that these fictional characters represent multitudes of real people, north and south of the Rio Grande. John represents those who think of liberation theology as just another confirmation of the stereotype that Latin America is the place of wars and rumors of wars. Rosa Maria's own country, Nicaragua, has been embroiled in bloody turmoil. Thousands of teenagers took to the battle, and hundreds died. Her home city, Leon, was a battleground

to match anything from World War II. So her words are
not empty slogans, but an accurate expression of a current
milieu.

John will return to managing his investments, thinking
all the while that his capitalism will, in the long run, help
more people than any military or socialistic venture. Rosa
Maria will return to her political action that expresses her
"obedience of faith." Was there, in this dialogue, any
communication across the Rio Grande?

In the closing pages of this chapter, I will affirm a
number of elements in the dialogue, as well as point out
several unresolved questions in my mind.

(1) Liberation theology is calling all of us to recognize
once again that *theory* and *practice* must be integrated.
Faith without works is dead. Works without faith is
devious. Further, we can learn from the liberationists that
in the praxis and *because of the praxis* one's faith can be
made "more intelligent." In educational circles these
days, one hears the word *heurism*, or *heuristic method*. It
refers to that process of inquiry in which the student
creates new methods and uses new tools that are called for
by the strange problems he/she encounters in the
inquiry. One can't predict beforehand what will take
place "out there," so one must be prepared to learn by
doing. In some ways, the road of faith and works is
heuristic, for a process of development takes place *on the
road*.

(2) The discussion between John and Rosa Maria
reminds us that religion is two dimensional—the vertical
and the horizontal. "Master, what must I do to inherit
eternal life?" Jesus replied with a question, "What is
written in the Law?" The lawyer answered, "Love the
Lord your God with all your heart, with all your soul, with

all your strength, and with all your mind; and your neighbour as yourself." Jesus pressed the lawyer to recognize two dimensions of spiritual concern — vertical relations with God, and horizontal ties with neighbors. The Anglo-Saxon, Protestants according to Rosa Maria, emphasize the former. The Latins, according to John, emphasize the latter. Most of us have failed to develop a holistic religious "field."

(3) Theology willy-nilly reflects the larger milieu in which theologians work. So it is that any academic theory reflects the sociology or psychology or journalism or science of the day. And we would do well to "raise the curtain" on that milieu time and again to recognize the distinct shape and size of our "learning." It is unfair to charge that Latin American theologians are "taken in" by their cultural milieu, assuming all the while that European and North American theologians are above the cultural fray.

(4) Rosa Maria is correct, I'm sorry to admit, that the typical university student of Latin America receives a broader general education than the typical university student of the United States. Our general education is West-oriented. We are strong on experimental science but weak on speculative science. We cover U.S. literature and perhaps British literature, but seldom consider the art from the East or the Third World. In the social sciences, history has taken a backseat to social psychology. Philosophy and political science remain on the outskirts of the general education curriculum.

(5) Although we Western democrats often sing the praises of freedom, I don't think we can overemphasize the beauty and power of this unmatchable privilege. Socialism, in its justifiable concern for all humanity, has

yet to achieve the right blending of freedom and responsibility.

(6) Finally, and most importantly, the debate about liberation theology serves notice to people such as John Smith and me that despite our pious concerns for those "less fortunate than we are," many of us North American Christians haven't made effective contact with the poor nor exerted ourselves on their behalf. We have not made the welfare of the poor our first option. Many of us still think of "the other" as an angel unawares who stumbles across our path, rather than someone whose values we learn and whose cultural categories we take on ourselves, someone whose struggles become our struggles. Many of us North American Christians are thoroughly and permanently isolated from the death-dealing horrors of the world. And, in fact, we may even unconsciously contribute to the problem.

So much for affirmations. My brief study of liberation theology has left me with many unresolved questions. I will list several of them.

(1) When and how does Jesus' kingdom come? John Smith thinks it comes through conversion and holy living and faith in a future reign of God in heaven. Rosa Maria fights for the kingdom to come even now on earth, in material and physical form.

(2) How does the theological process right itself? If European theology is near-sighted, if North American theology is secular, if Latin American theology is politicized, how can correctives be introduced into the process? In other words, how can theologians truly apprehend the Spirit moving upon the face of the earth?

(3) *Laisse faire* capitalism, as outlined by Adam Smith, has given a license to the powerful to exploit the weak.

Socialism, as outlined by Marx and Engels, levels out the differences of human potential. Why do those who debate liberation theology insist on one or the other of these nineteenth-century political philosophies, untempered by the adaptations brought on by twentieth-century realities? And why do even Christians, after opting for a political persuasion, follow it so uncritically?

(Pope John Paul II has contributed significantly to the discussion of Christianity and politics, to the extent that some observers conclude that "The pope emphatically reject(s) liberation theology." To be sure, at Puebla Mexico, he rejected atheistic humanism as a source of Christian liberation inasmuch as economic determinism eclipses spiritual dynamics. More pointedly, he indicated that Marxist revolutionary tactics, based on class conflict, violate Christian teaching. He spoke out about the so-called political Jesus: "People claim to show Jesus as politically committed, as one who fought against Roman oppression and the authorities and also as one involved in the class struggle. This idea of Christ as a political figure, a revolutionary, as the subversive man from Nazareth, does not tally with the church's catechesis." [60]

While such statements encouraged church conservatives in Latin America who opposed liberation theology, the pope did not hesitate to align himself with the very issues that produced a liberation theology in the first place. He spoke out again and again on behalf of human rights, called for economic justice and the redistribution of land, attacked the powerful rich classes, defended laborers' rights, and even supported those who migrate in search of work. In his encyclica, "The Redemption of Man," he deplored the political domination—be it totalitarianism, neocolonialism, imperialism—that condemns people to suffering.)

(4) In recent years, theologians and sociologists have become aware in a new way that the entire Latin

American region has been *continually* oppressed since
the first *conquistadores* landed. The inclination of the
scholars is to search out and reprimand the oppressor. But
might there not be indigenous or endemic characteristics
that make the region attractive to oppressors? Bruno
Bettelheim, in his widely read analyses of the holocaust in
Nazi Germany, suggested that a scholar who wishes to
study the dynamics of persecution should pay close
attention not only to the persecutor but also to the
persecuted. Has Latin America brought oppression onto
itself?

(5) Multinational companies are charged with much of
the evil-doings in Latin America. Many critics are now
saying that these huge conglomerates, rather than state
governments, are running the Third World. How,
precisely, does a multinational company exploit a nation?

(6) And finally, it seems to me—as an outside
observer—that the political option many Latin American
youth are choosing is actually neither capitalism nor
socialism but anarchism. That option strikes me as
particularly incongruous with the notion of an efficacious
faith. What has been the history of anarchist movements?
To what extent have they produced liberation? Why is
anarchism a tempting option for youth?

This chapter has been about theology. The reader may
remember that our John Smith said, "I think of theology
as a conscious discourse about God, His will, and His
work in heaven and earth." And Rosa Maria added her
perspective, "I think of theology as a conscious effort to
make possible the life that God wanted all people to
have." Those two statements may reveal a rather stark
contrast in understanding, even among disciples of Jesus
Christ.

But Jesus was talking to His disciples as well as to John and Rose Maria when He told them this is how they should pray:

> Our Father in heaven,
> thy name be hallowed;
> thy kingdom come,
> thy will be done,
> on earth as in heaven.
> Give us today our daily bread.
> Forgive us the wrong we have done,
> as we have forgiven those who have wronged us.
> And do not bring us to the test,
> but save us from the evil one.
> For thine is the kingdom and the power and the glory,
> for ever.
> Amen.

In praying that model prayer, the Spirit may hear and answer needs of which we in our blindness of perspective are not even aware.

Wetbacks

*A review of the factors that cause illegal
immigration to the United States, and a
reflection on U.S. responses to this
"invasion"*

You have had your own opinions about the Iron Curtain
for a long time. But, what do you think of the "Tortilla
Curtain?"

The Tortilla Curtain is the nickname of a proposed
fence for two sections of the border between the United
States and Mexico. In October of 1978, the U.S.
Immigration and Naturalization Service (INS) announced
the construction of the barrier for about six and a half
miles in the area where El Paso, Texas, borders the
Mexican city of Juarez, and for another six miles at the
Pacific Ocean near Chula Vista, California.

The curtain is to be quite sturdy. First there would be a
concrete base, set several feet into the earth to discourage
any tunneling under it. Next would come a five-foot wall
of galvanized steel heavy enough to withstand ordinary
cutting torches. On the top would be about six feet of

tightly woven chain links with razor sharp edges to repel any climbers.

Cost estimates for the construction and installation of the fence range from $1.4 million to $3.5 million. If the fence does its job well, the length may be extended, officials explained.

Several Undebatable Facts

Such projects produce strong opinions. No sooner did the INS announce the construction than editorial writers made comparisons with the China wall, the Roman wall in northern England, and the Berlin Wall. Others invoked the wisdom of Robert Frost about good fences making good neighbors; a few deliberately misquoted Frost, insisting that good fences do not make good neighbors.

The debates will not soon end. In fact, the general public will continue the discussions until a public sentiment is formed. Before we get involved in the discussion in this chapter, let us pause to examine several facts that everybody on both sides of the fence-to-be-built can accept as verifiable.

Fact 1: The border between the United States and Mexico stretches for 1,950 miles, beginning between Brownsville and Matamoros at the Gulf of Mexico, following the Rio Grande northwestward to El Paso/Juarez, then leaving the river and heading westward, missing the Gulf of California and crowning Baja California before ending at the Pacific Ocean near Chula Vista.

Fact 2: Despite the power grabs, the injustices, the exploitations, the boundary disputes, the intrigues and takeovers that write the history of U.S./Mexican relations, the two countries are friendly to each other. There is relatively easy passage from one country to the other—that is, for legal travelers. The border has its guards and checkpoints, but one wouldn't call the border a belt of bullets.

Fact 3: Years ago the U.S. immigration quotas favored European countries. Now in more recent years there has been a great influx of Hispanic peoples. In just five years, the Hispanic-American community increased by 14.3 percent, totalling today about 12,000,000![1]

Fact 4: In addition to the millions of legal immigrants in the U.S. today, there are many illegal aliens. Ninety percent of illegal Hispanics come from Mexico. The actual number is unknown. The federal government admits to the figure of 8,000,000. The aliens themselves put their number at 19,000,000.

Fact 5: In 1977 the INS apprehended, in a kind of cat-and-mouse game, about 1,000,000 aliens and deported them back to Mexico. But because of the length of the boundary between the countries and the somewhat relaxed guard of the border, many of those expelled persons immediately return. It is thought that 1,000,000 persons are crossing illegally each year.

An alien is a person who enters without a proper visa, work permit, or passport. Since he or she cannot enter at a checkpoint, the emigrant must somehow cross somewhere else. Many, of course, cross the Rio Grande where it is shallow. (How many have drowned is unknown.) As the border guard has increased its vigilance, the would-be immigrants have devised more ingenious ways of crossing: in trunks and motors and seats of cars, tied under cars and trucks, in boats and airplanes, and even in the underground drainage pipes that link Tijuana, Mexico, and Chula Vista, California. As one would expect, such illegal activity invites charlatans. A network of people-smugglers charge from $200 to $500 for underground "ferry service."

Other Assertions

In most disputations, everyone knows about and accepts a common body of information. And in most disputations there is a body of information *not* commonly shared—facts that are unknown, possibly inaccessible, possibly guarded by one side, possibly rejected as being incompatible with an already formed opinion, possibly embarrassing or incriminating. Surely in the disputations about aliens who don't carry proper documents, one can find many facts of this second kind. Let us sample some of these items, which we shall label with the term "Assertions."

> *Assertion 1:* By far the majority of the illegal aliens from Mexico are poorer, less educated, less skilled, less cultured (in the sense of refinement) than the typical resident of the United States.
> *Assertion 2:* The jobs they do are usually hard, dirty, and unattractive to the typical U.S. laborer.
> *Assertion 3:* Although there are wage laws in the United States, many illegal aliens receive far lower than minimum wages. Many are not covered by pension plans and worker's compensation.
> *Assertion 4:* Because the illegal alien can be apprehended and deported, he must live a somewhat clandestine life, in fear of being caught. Further, he or she must absorb a lot of hostilities, from uncaring employers, from labor unions, and possibly most painful of all, from legal Mexican immigrants.
> *Assertion 5:* Despite these problems, the illegal alien finds life much better in the United States than in his/her native Mexico.

These facts and assertions point to a tremendous problem in international relations. While a ready solution to the problem is not obvious, many of us will soon form an opinion about the problem. What interests us in this book is that the opinion we adopt, which we will esteem as our own unique creation, will actually be little more than the "insights" impressed upon us by our own limited frame of reference. That is, we will see things from our point of view. The illegal aliens will see things from another point of view. Our arguments will make sense to those who see things as we do. The arguments of the aliens will look quite ridiculous to us, but of course not to them.

As was stated in the preface of this book, we are not trying to destroy the variety of points of view. But we are unapologetically calling for people to take a second look, even to the extent of considering the vantage point of the other person—to stand where he or she stands and view the larger panorama.

We will try to help the reader achieve this broader perspective by introducing two persons in such a way that their attitudes and opinions about illegal aliens become transparencies of their particular frames of reference. By studying their attitudes and their ways of expressing those attitudes, the reader may be able to decipher some of the sources of his own attitudes.

The two persons will be fabricated from impressions I have received from direct encounters, reading, data from reports, and my own imagination. Any resemblance to any person living or dead in the United States or Mexico is not at all coincidental, because I've tried to make them as similar as possible to various people I know.

One will be a resident of northern Indiana, whom we will call Mrs. Anna Kauffman, age 48.

The other will be an illegal alien from the Mexican state of Oaxaca, whom we will call Sr. Jose Gonzalez, age 28.

What follows are only their words, in response to an "interview" with me. In that interview I have asked them pointed questions about illegal aliens, and they have kindly given pointed answers.

Mrs. Anna Kauffman

. . . You can call me what you want. Even Mrs. Archie Bunker. Ha, ha. No, I'll tell you frankly, I'm not a prejudiced person. Opinionated, sure as can be, but not prejudiced.

. . . Don't give me a quiz about Latin America or I'll fail, and my feelings can be hurt, you know! It would just give you more to write about. It's south of the Rio Grande river, we learned in grade school. I'm not defending my ignorance. No I'm not. I'm just saying that I'm a resident of the U.S. and I can tell Oregon from Ohio, but don't ask me to tell you about Mexico or Argentina.

. . . I can tell from your grin that you think I'm a closed-minded senior citizen from the Bible Belt looking for something to fuss about. You're wrong on every count. I'm not a senior citizen and if you want to see my birth certificate, I'll show you. I might be fussy, but I'm fussy about good things. Pretty things, for example. I'm sure Mexico has its pretty things too. I'm sure there are thousands of people there who like nice things. And those people would fuss too if wetbacks destroyed their things.

. . . Don't you think intelligent people usually want to fit in? Honestly now, don't you think so? If you moved to London, wouldn't you want to have an English garden? If you lived in Venice, wouldn't you ride the boats? If you lived in China, wouldn't you eat with chopsticks? Then tell me, why don't the Mexicans in this town keep a decent lawn?

. . . Melting pot? What are you talking about? You want to make this an academic discussion, and I already told you I surprised everyone by finishing high school. Okay, this country was a melting pot. This country took in more than one boatload of forlorn travelers. But at some point the pot gets full, don't you know, and then the pot boils over and you have a mess. And we're in that mess right now.

. . . And when those Mexican kids take their full fists into the milk store five times a day, what do they buy? What do they

buy? Toothrotters, that's what they buy. Toothrotters. And
then United Way is supposed to set up free dental clinics, ha,
ha, ha. I laugh only when the joke is funny.

. . . You are taunting me. I am not prejudiced. The same
good Lord made us all. What I'm talking about is not dark or
light skin, but a simple respect for law. You either have law or
you don't. The people I'm complaining about are breakers of
law. They have come into our country without having the
proper papers. If I went into their country without a passport,
I'd be as guilty as they.

. . . People say, "Be patient. Mexicans will adapt like other
immigrants adapted." Why don't you ask Mr. Lockert about his
patience? He's the one who was in the accident up on Route 20.
Mrs. Lockert was killed. A Mexican, without a driver's license,
speeding, passed on a hill and hit the Lockerts head on. We
came upon the scene before an ambulance got there, and the
Mexican just sat on the road bank and didn't have a thing to say.

. . . Slaughtering chickens isn't a good job, I'll grant you that.
I had to do it as a child. Cut off the heads, pick the feathers, and
remove the insides. And in Martin's slaughterhouse, the heat
and the smell are not pleasant. Martin probably couldn't find
local people to do it for what he can pay. So I guess we can thank
them for that.

. . . Just look, will you, at the house by the milk store. It was
once a beautiful residence. Now broken windows, the door
always hanging open. Junk in the yard. Two or three cars out
front — one always on blocks, another without a muffler — rusted
out. And there are people in and out of there all day long! I
mean all day long. I honestly can't tell you who the residents
are, because people are coming and going. One of the
neighbors wondered if it might be a house of ill repute, but I
said no the police wouldn't allow it. But between you and me, I
doubt very much if those women are married, and just about all
the people who stop in are men.

. . . And so Harriet and I just don't talk much about it. If her
husband wants to work at Su Amigo, who am I to argue? But as I
was saying, Harriet told me that when the government officials
check out the poultry plant, the Mexicans drop everything —
even chickens half gutted, and run for the cornfields. They

know they're here illegally. But Martin turns around and gives them work, and Su Amigo—it just serves as a haven for them.

. . . Our children went to Chadwell School, yes. But that was before the Mexican invasion, if you'll pardon the expression. In those days parents fought to get their children into Chadwell, and nowadays they fight to get them transferred out. Samuel Higgins ran a tight ship, that's for sure. But you can't blame the kids for the playground fights, and the dirty clothes. They're here a week or a month, then move on. They don't speak English, but I didn't get A's in it either. Hey, look over at the house. There's another man entering, and it's what, 10:30 in the morning? What's this, coffee break at Martin's Poultry?

. . . First Church is NOT to be thanked for anything. Okay, they gave the old building to the Mexicans, but then huh, they move to the west side, and we are left with a Mexican church and Mexican neighbors and you can guess what's happening to our real estate values.

. . . The Catholic Church had the bazaar for Su Amigo, and how could I be a hypocrite and go? I don't like Su Amigo anymore than I like hot tacos.

. . . I'm not a bashful person. But I am honest. I say what's on my mind. If you were an illegal Mexican, I'd tell you to your face that breaking the law is wrong, wrong, wrong. Did you write that down?

. . . What makes a good community? What do you want, a politician's speech? You won't get that here with your coffee. I'm no politician, just a citizen who didn't go beyond high school. You know what a good community is as well as I. It's people who care. And there are people who care and those who don't. Those who care work hard to make a place decent. Those who don't care usually prefer to live across the Penn Central tracks. Okay, I'll accept that this town has its poor section, even though it's no honor to have a slum in town. But my dander gets up when they move in here.

. . . No, I talk too loud. I guess it's not a crisis. The mayor would not have to call in the national guard! This county has maybe a thousand wetbacks, according to Harriet. Now if we were like some counties in Texas and California—I've seen on TV whole towns that are—what would you call them,

Mexico-on-the-road. Now, that's a crisis if those people are here illegally. In twenty years from now? Maybe all the Mexicans will come here, and my grandchildren will go and make a place to live in empty Mexico! Now that's something for you to write down!

. . . I'm glad a hundred times Henry's no merchant. Sure, he comes home covered with paint from hair to toenails, but I'd take that over the problems of the merchant. What the Mexicans do, is a bunch will go together and put a down payment on a big color TV. Then they'll all watch it, but not make more payments. Now which of the fifty men does the merchant collect from? They all deny that they own it. By the time the collection agency is authorized to take back the television, the merchant loses his money and the television is a damaged piece of merchandise.

. . . Mrs. Lambright hit the nail on the head. She said that 10 percent of the population claims 90 percent of the doctor's time. That's about it, right on the nose. A couple of people make enough trouble for everyone. Who are the ones brought into the emergency room after midnight? Nine chances in ten, it's the migrants who get to drinking their paychecks. And the doctor stitches them up and sends them to the office and there they are too drunk to talk and too broke to pay. So our room rates go up to pay off those bad bills.

. . . So if you don't want more coffee, and you don't have more questions, just mark me down as in love with the human race but not too hep on these illegal Mexicans.

Before going on to the profile of Sr. Jose Gonzalez, you may wish to reread the statements by Mrs. Kauffman and from them begin to reconstruct the history, the values, and the priorities in the life of Mrs. Kauffman and her neighbors. To assist you in that process, here are a number of lead-questions:

1. What is Mrs. Kauffman's net economic worth? What is the value of her house? What other economic assets has she?

How did she get these assets? Inheritance? Investments?
Hard work? Saving? Stealing?

2. Which institutions of society does Mrs. Kauffman value
most highly? Which ones does she depreciate?

3. Put in your own words Mrs. Kauffman's attitude about
culture and education?

4. Mrs. Kauffman denied that she could define what is a
good community, but she was defining it all through her
responses. What is her definition of good community?

5. What does Mrs. Kauffman have to lose by the coming of
strangers? Put these items in personal perspective.

6. What are the values that Mrs. Kauffman thinks her
community will lose with the coming of strangers? Put these
items into social perspective.

Sr. Jose Gonzalez

. . . Payday! Payday! That is why I am here. Payday pleases
me very much. When there is money in the pocket, and a
señorita on the arm, then there is a cheerful song in the heart!

. . . Yes, yes, I like everything here. It is a beautiful country,
a large rich land of many pleasures. Here there are stores and
cheap merchandise and food and cars. The people here do not
have to worry about anything, not anything.

. . . Very well, very well. Yes very well. Mr. Martin is a good
man, he pays very well. We have no complaints. He is very
friendly, and when he gets angry about something, he is right to
be angry. We Mexicans can get lazy sometimes. Mr. Martin is
the best employer I know. *Ay dios mio,* you don't know the
brutes who hire *los indocumentados* (undocumented aliens).
People without shame. One boss in Texas says he pays every
two weeks, so I took work there. When payday arrived, the
police came to the factory and captured us. Strange, on the
payday! It was the boss, the shameless one, who always calls the
police so that he doesn't have to pay *los indocumentados.*

. . . We *indocumentados* all have nicknames. We don't use
our real names and surnames. What do you think of mine?
"Trotamundo" (The Globetrotter). They gave it to me because
I've made five trips back to Mexico—but not on Pan Am jets like
the famous Globetrotters use! I got caught by the police. Some

say it is bad luck, but I don't believe that. It's my fault. When I have money in my pocket, I get very happy and go out and celebrate like a vagabond and then I talk too much or go to places that are dangerous and *caray*! I'm sitting handcuffed in a police car heading in a direction opposite the needle of a compass! That's life. One time was very unpleasant. I was being beaten by a group of union workers in a cannery and my head was cracked open like a coconut, so I was taken to a hospital in an ambulance. A nice fast ride. But in the hospital they found out I was undocumented. They bandaged my head, but then sent me south, carrying nothing but a big headache!

 . . . No, I am not a drunkard. No, my father was an alcoholic and his father was an alcoholic and when he beat up on me and my mother I decided to be careful. I take a drink, and maybe once a month we will have a big party on payday, but we stay in the cabins at the Plant   [Martin's Poultry]. We don't go out on the streets like fools.

 . . . The cabin is the nicest house I have ever lived in. I don't understand the complaints you make. College people come and ask us questions about the cabins. Government people go in and search around without asking our permission. Church people say Mr. Martin isn't a Christian because he gives us such houses. What are they saying? Our cabin pleases us all. I am not saying this just to defend Mr. Martin. Our cabin pleases us all. And if we ask for something more, we get it. Do you know, Mr. Martin, who is very busy, comes at least once a month to check on the stove and we say don't worry about the stove and don't listen to the college people and the government people and the church people. We are very happy. *Dios mio*, what would they say if they saw where *mi mujer* (my woman) lives in Mexico!

 . . . You are like the college people. *Gringos* ask questions and fill many questionnaires! Is it your hobby? I wonder, do *gringos* ask questions of their women?

 . . . Life was hard in Mexico, what more can I say? The mother of my children is searching garbage cans today. I send her money, but often the letters are opened. If I could take money back when I get caught, I would gladly go. Someday I will pay a smuggler to bring her here. But she will miss her mother, that is sure.

. . . Many, many jobs I tried in Mexico, but there one works for nothing. Hunger never goes away. I like to make *rascas*. Do you know *rascas*? You have a big block of ice, you have a ice plane to chip off ice. Then you put the ice in a paper cone and top it with milk and syrup. It is hard work, first walking three kilometers to rent a cart, then pushing the cart across the town to the ice factory, and then pushing it to the playground or the factory. That's the problem—finding the place. And of course getting money to rent the cart and buy the ice and toppings. If you don't have a place, you can push the cart all day. Others have places and hire boys to beat up anyone who takes the place. If I would have had money each day to rent the cart and buy the ice, I could have had a place, but as it was, I'd end up in some poor neighborhood where the children had no money and they would beg and beg all day until the ice melted and I would finally give them *rascas* and lose all my profit. I would push the cart all the way back to the shop and walk home thinking of the kids I made happy so that I wouldn't think of what *mi mujer* would say. There were many jobs, but *rascas* was the best. I wanted to drive a bus, but tell me, how can one get a job like that when one is poor?

. . . No, I do not go to the church. Sometimes people from the Protestant churches come to the cabins on Sunday to give programs, but I leave because I am not a Protestant and they just come in without asking. One time in Texas a priest came to our houses, and heard our confessions and gave us communion. But that is one priest in a thousand. No priest in this area would go to the cabins to give communion.

. . . Yes, of course, I would want my children to be here. Then they would not get hungry. I would give them a dollar every day to go to the store to buy what they want. They have never bought what they want. What is a *peso* able to buy? And who has an extra *peso*?

. . . Yes, it is hard to find our kinds of food. Some stores have good rice, but we can't always find our type of beans. One time church people decided to give us a *fiesta*. All of the farm workers. It was kind of them to propose a *fiesta*, but what a *fiesta*. No music! Only a preacher who talked in very bad Spanish. And then food, but strange food. They gave us each a paper plate and things like orange juice, carrots, pickles, sandwiches of tasteless meat, sweet beans with ketchup. They were kind people but they didn't know what we like to eat!

. . . I do not know the neighbors but they are nice. They do not bother us. They are always busy, so they do not stop to talk. Of course, they don't talk Spanish, and we talk English like chickens.

. . . We don't agree here about Su Amigo. They are nice people, but they ask too many questions and write down the answers. Some day, those answers will begin talking, if you know what I mean. We need a place like Su Amigo to help us get loans from the bank, to help us find out if we paid too much taxes, to help us get documents, to help us get driver's licenses. Some of the Mexicans won't talk with them, but I do. They are nice people. But you remember. I am the *Trotamundo* because I talk too much!

. . . you are right, we should have our women here. There are fights sometimes, but you can't blame the *machos*. In Mexico we knew where we could find the women, but here it is different. If an *indocumentado* goes into South Bend to find a woman, he is asking for trouble. But we are men; we need our women here.

. . . The tortilla curtain is nothing. Don't we have legs? Can't we walk to areas where there is no fence? The fence is just the funny way of government.

Again, the reader may wish to probe beneath the facade, to understand Jose as a human being.

1. What gives Jose a sense of well-being?

2. Which needs are being met now that were not being met in Mexico?

3. By what criteria does Jose judge people?

4. Summarize his attitudes about religion. About government.

5. What is behind his several comments about questions being asked and answers written down?

6. How might Jose answer the question, "What makes a community a good one?"

7. Describe his impression of people like Mrs. Kauffman.
8. Does he reveal a sense of personal and social responsibility? Explain.

The reader may also profit from comparing attitudes of Mrs. Kauffman and Sr. Jose Gonzalez. This might be done by completing the matrix below:

attitude concerning . . .	Mrs. Kauffman	Sr. Gonzalez
Mr. Martin		
buying food at the milk store		
role of Su Amigo		
dressing chickens		
living quarters, church houses		
sexual relations		

Through the responses of Mrs. Kauffman and Sr. Gonzalez we begin to perceive the limited vision of any one person in this large international problem. And if 10,000,000 persons are affected by the construction of a Tortilla Curtain, there will be 10,000,000 individual experiences and millions of different frames of reference.

If one could merely pass it all off with, "How interesting that different people have different points of view!" But we can't do that, knowing full well that the issue of undocumented aliens has in the past provoked prejudice, exploitation, and even war. Two examples give more than enough evidence: In 1937 President Trujillo of the Dominican Republic ordered the expulsion of Haitians who had, over a number of years, crossed over the border to work in Dominican plantations. The order led to a massacre in which 10,000 to 20,000 Haitians were killed. In 1969 El Salvador and Honduras fought a bitter one-week war because more than 600,000 Salvadorans had fled their overpopulated and impoverished land to settle in Honduras. Diplomatic relations have still not been resumed between these Central American neighbors.

All one needs to do is look at some of the recent proposals for solving the wetback invasion to foresee increased tension:

—to build a fence the entire length of the border.
—to fine, as does Germany, any employer who knowingly hires an illegal alien.
—to increase surveillance of the border through helicopters, guards, and electronic sensors.

Meanwhile, the people-smugglers will be charging higher and higher fees to get more and more persons into the United States.

Little wonder, then, that Leonel J. Castillo, a Carter-appointed commissioner of the U.S. Immigration and Naturalization Service, would say, "Among the many questions that confront the United States in regards to the other Americas—the Panama Canal, human rights, economic development, population increase, energy conservation—I think that none is more important than immigration. All of the others are related to it." [2]

The Larger Vision

I believe that our own understanding of this critical dilemma could be increased through two "lenses"—one for allowing a larger view, and the other for encouraging a more humane view. Let us deal with the former first, for it establishes a frame of reference for the second.

When I refer to a larger view, I am indicating a panorama that encompasses a longer period of time and a greater amount of territory. It is helpful to consider a universe larger than the daily activities of Mrs. Kauffman and Sr. Gonzalez. And the period of time must transcend a day or a year from their lives.

Let's begin with the question *why?* Why do people pick up and move to another place illegally? Sometimes they do it to escape political persecution. Sometimes there are religious, tribal, or language wars. But usually—in the vast majority of cases—people migrate to find work (and consequently food, clothing, and shelter).

Where does this happen? Movements in search of work (and life) have brought millions of people from rural areas to urban areas, but of course those movements have not really solved the problem. Now, news that life is better in another country and easier transportation have triggered international migrations. A dramatic example in recent years has been the migration of thousands of south Sahara people of Africa, driven from their homes by drought, into other African countries which can ill afford to feed them. But this is only one example. The India-Pakistan-Bangladesh migrations offer another modern case. In Latin America, Argentina is currently "carrying" about 600,000 Bolivians, and Venezuela has been invaded by about the same number of Colombians. In other words, illegal migrations can be found all over the world.

The incentive for international migration, prompted by hunger, can be expressed quite graphically in the case of the United States and Mexico. The population of the United States was estimated to be 224.2 million in mid-1978. Its per capita income reported for 1975 was $7,060. In the six most populated countries of Latin America (including Mexico), approximately the same number of people—207 million—have a per capita income of $75 a year. In other words, Mrs. Kauffman has probably been receiving 100 times more income in Indiana than Sr. Gonzalez in Mexico.[3]

At a time in 1978 when the unemployment in the United States was hovering above 6 percent (and disturbing the Carter administration), 50 percent of Mexico's work force had no employment! [4]

The rate of population growth from the years 1970 to 1974 in the United States had fallen to .8 percent. Meanwhile, Mexico had one of the highest rates in the world—4.2 percent. It has since reduced its rate to 3.5 percent but even at this rate, the population of Mexico will double in just 22 years! [5] By the turn of the century, Mexico City is likely to be the largest city of the world.

The devaluation of the peso and rising inflation rates have driven up the price of a piece of bread in Mexico. When a person is starving, he looks anywhere for food.

If this problem seems critical now, what shall be the size of the problem our children face, when, by the year 2000, Latin America will need to maintain all of its current jobs and add an additional 100,000 job opportunities?

Not until Planet Earth can solve its basic problem of feeding its people will illegal migrations be stopped. Is there any wall anywhere however thick and high that can take away hunger pains?

The solution to hunger will likely not come from one person, one agency, or one country. In fact, it won't come from one group of nations—even the rich industrial nations. What further evidence of aborted economic planning do we need than the failure of the "decades of progress" in Latin America?

Nor will the solution be found in a simple channeling of money or other resources from rich nations to poor nations. The Marshall Plan may have rebuilt war-torn Europe, and World Bank loans may have temporarily stimulated local development, but there is little evidence to support the long-range efficacy of handouts from rich to poor.

And it is my opinion that political revolution itself will not solve the harsh inequalities of the haves and the have-nots. Tyranny, prompted by greed, can be enthroned in both democratic and socialistic systems. It is too easy to say that a change in government will solve all of our problems.

While I am not qualified to propose solutions or even participate intelligently in the hunger-solving debates, I can summarize what the experts perceive to be some of the elements that must go into the final solution. Expressed in lay language, world hunger will not be solved until . . .

(1) *All leaders of the world engage in solving the problem.* Until we work on an international scale, our proposals will be too localized and self-serving to reach the deep and pervasive problems that cause hunger. All the nations of the Americas must be involved in the Argentinian/Bolivian migrations, the Venezuelan/Colombian migrations, the Mexican/United States migrations, and others.

(2) *People come to see personal and national rewards in a common worldwide fight against hunger.* Essential economic change will not be brought about just by wishing it, nor by philanthropy, nor by charity. This is a difficult saying for the "do-gooders" who believe their works of kindness to be the extent of their responsibility. Fundamental economic change will occur only when people allow it to happen, and they won't allow it to happen until there are personal and immediate awards for them. People are, after all, human beings who seek out gratification!

(3) *Centers of production are placed in areas of greatest efficiency and where employment potential is greatest.* John Cole of the *London Observer* [6] has boldly suggested that certain industries such as textiles, shoes, leathers, electric productions, and more should gradually be moved into Third World countries, closer to raw materials and a work force. At present, production is held by a few entrepreneurs, and centered in technological cases. Raw materials move from Third World countries to the production centers, thus assuring an impoverished producer and an enriched manufacturer.

(4) *Distribution of goods is worldwide.* National self-interest has erected fences larger than any Tortilla Curtain. I refer to the barriers to free trade. As each country tries to protect its own industries, it shuts out products that compete with homemade products. As one country's tariff responds to another country's tariff, and one restriction butts against another restriction, the goods of the world are held back from those who need them most.

(5) *Resources are conserved.* Conservation has many facets that we are still unacquainted with: using each raw

material completely and most efficiently, consuming no more than one needs, disposing of wastes in a manner that does not damage life, rebuilding depleted resources, learning to discontinue using resources in low supply, sharing resources across national boundaries, and so forth.

(6) *Common people are enlisted by their leaders to help in this concerted effort.* Any proposals for solving hunger remain only idealistic formulations until all people are participating in hunger-solution.

In summary, the larger view gives to us a more complete picture of the dynamics of hunger that cause the illegal migrations. After looking carefully at that picture we lose the innocence of our provincialism, and possibly even some of our bias.

The Humane Vision

Attitudes are formed from the stuff of our personal experience, from our interaction with others, and from what we learn secondhanded. In the case of Mrs. Anna Kauffman, her negative attitude toward illegal aliens is a "natural" product of her less-than-rewarding experiences with the Mexican farm laborers, and of her conversations with friends. (The information gleaned from Harriet troubles Mrs. Kauffman, for Harriet's husband is working on behalf of the illegal aliens. Mrs. Kauffman conveniently removes herself from that information.) Not until Mrs. Kauffman—and all of us—sees the larger picture can there be much hope in the re-forming of attitudes.

We must eventually recognize that the people who move illegally into our towns, although they be acting out their own wills, are nonetheless victims of circumstances. If Jose Gonzalez and his friends were not in northern

Indiana, there would be others, because the circumstances of unemployment produce migration. That fact will not go away.

And we must recognize that the circumstance of unemployment with its resulting hunger is not just Mexico's problem. All of us are implicated in some way. We would do well to discover some of the ways that we are directly related to Mexico's poverty. (Which of our food products are protected by tariffs so that Mexico's product can't compete with ours? Which of our manufactured products have used raw materials from Mexico, and now that the products are manufactured, are too expensive for Mexicans to buy? How many North American companies that we own stock in pay us our dividends from the profits extracted from Mexican plants?)

Such recognitions should bring us to a more appropriate response of compassion. Unfortunately, the word *compassion* is likely to call forth our almost instinctive Protestant response of giving more charity, but that is not what is needed. We Christians are conditioned to the idea of giving "an offering" to the poor. "But if a man has enough to live on, and yet when he sees his brother in need shuts up his heart against him, how can it be said that the divine love dwells in him? (1 John 3:17). I should wish to argue, however, that there are forms of compassion better than the North American "handout." (In too many cases, free gifts inflate the ego of the giver and debilitate the receiver.)

What might be some more appropriate responses of compassion that we North Americans might make toward illegal aliens? We assume, of course, that these responses of compassion do not solve the long-range hunger and unemployment problem, but rather serve to humanize the situation until the problem is solved.

Does it mean, for example, that we should oppose the Tortilla Curtain? Not necessarily. I personally hope that the Imigration and Naturalization Service does not build a 2,000-mile fence. On the other hand, I can understand the need to limit the migration of a million people each year, for the benefit of both the migrators and the country to which they go.

I would briefly cite ten specific humane responses that I've heard about, any one of which the U.S. citizen might identify with.

(1) We should urge the U.S. government to appoint people to the Imigration and Naturalization Service who have the larger vision, and a response of compassion in this problem. President Carter has already appointed Leonel Castillo to the INS. His grandfather was an illegal alien.

(2) Counseling centers should be set up in every population of illegal aliens to provide a setting where the aliens can get information and guidance for solving their many problems. These centers do not have to be government-run. In fact, churches and civic groups might operate them under the blessing of the INS.

(3) Elementary schools located in populations of illegal aliens should offer a special education coordinator to receive the children of the aliens, and to address the unique problems of learning that these children bring. If the school system cannot support this staff member, other civic groups or individuals might foot the bill.

(4) Church boards should establish minority ministries — not a mission to the minorities, but a facilitating of their own religious expression.

(5) So long as there is not a law against hiring aliens, employers should delineate jobs for aliens that do not jeopardize the positions of citizens.

(6) Inasmuch as illegal aliens are "locked into" job

responsibilities in which no healthy escape is available for them emotionally and physically, community recreation services ought to look for ways of incorporating the aliens into summer athletic programs, town festivals, fairs, and recreation.

(7) The United States never *gave* an easy assimilation to immigrants. As *Time* magazine has written, "In U.S. politics, representation by ethnic population is not handed out gratis, but must be fought for and won." So too, the Hispanic American immigrants must take on a political responsibility that involves hard work. They should be encouraged, by our political leaders, to begin the fight.

(8) Newspapers, TV, and radio stations, magazines, bulletins, and other media of communication ought to participate in the teaching of citizen responsibilities to immigrants. To own a house, to drive a car, to obtain a loan, to get an education, to gain the confidence of neighbors—all of these goals are reachable only if the seeker can sustain a discipline of his own actions. Immigrants, floating in the ecstasy of payday, must learn that payday is only one day in seven, and that life involves more than feeding a stomach.

(9) As the Hispanic American population increases, the United States must consider seriously bilingualism. Even small towns in northern Indiana should begin the two-language approach in education, in public signs, in mass communication, in religious activities.

(10) A clarification of housing codes is needed, possibly a revision that will allow a wider variety of low-income residences. Some of our codes enforce middle-income types of construction that are unreachable for many lower-class persons.

At a larger international—but no less immediate—level, the development of Mexico's vast oil holdings should elicit our interest. According to Mexico's national oil monopoly, PEMEX, the potential oil reserves in the Gulf of Mexico may total 300 billion barrels.[7] If that is true, Mexico, which had been importing its oil, would move ahead of Saudi Arabia as a petroleum giant.

What are the implications? Well, if Mexico can develop this natural resource in an efficient and productive manner, it may solve its internal employment problems quicker than we might have expected. But surely there are many trolls crouching beneath the surface of the waters! In the past, nations have not known how to assimilate large influxes of wealth without setting off inflation and waste. Second, it seems certain that a few entrepreneurs will grab a large portion of the wealth, while the masses will be deprived. The oil-producing countries illustrate the disparities and inequalities among the citizenry.

Of even greater concern to us should be the likelihood that these oil resources now belonging to Mexico will be exploited by the United States. We will benefit through the multinational companies who will extract favorable contracts with Mexico. We will get oil at cheaper prices. We will use the oil in our technological society. Meanwhile, Mexico will serve us. How can we circumvent that likelihood? Let us not put aside the question.

And finally, the humane vision should lead us away from the stereotypes of illegal aliens that permit us to "construct" a Jose Gonzalez, and that permit us to categorize millions of human beings as wetbacks, or Chicanos, or even Mexicans. Each is a human being who can enrich our lives as we enrich theirs. We are neighbors, after all, and a person no less than Jesus Christ wanted us to ponder the question, "Who is my neighbor?"

A Meeting

*A comparison of how four agencies of mass communication
handled news of the World Festival of Youth and Students in
Cuba during July and August, 1978*

I have been trying to show that people perceive their
world from a perspective that is limited by many kinds of
personal, social, and cultural blinders. Everyone has a
point of view. At least we ordinary human beings have
points of view—we who are ignorant and prejudiced,
impressionable and gullible.

But what about journalists? According to the tenets of
traditional journalism, the news reporter ought to do
better than "ordinary people." Journalists are trained to
perceive accurately, and to guard lest their own personal
feelings influence what they see. Let there be a grinding
auto crash: let there be twisted metal and flames of
gasoline; let there be groans, the starey gaze of shock, the
final gasp for air—but even these shouldn't keep a
journalist from conducting a cool, disinterested investiga-
tion. When the story appears in the newspaper, it should
read practically the same regardless of which of the

newspaper's reporters covered the accident.

Such is the "objectivity" of journalism. And there is good reason — so the argument runs — for journalists to be "unbiased." Are not opinions and attitudes based upon information? Are not public policies a response to the facts of contemporary life? If a people are not accurately and adequately informed, how can they think and respond wisely?

In the United States, we revere information so highly that the "right to know" is considered a moral necessity. And in a country that insists upon the right to know, the journalist carries a heavy responsibility not only to survey the whole world scape, but also to do it with precision and fairness.

We give passing grades to our United States journalists. To be sure, little errors slip into news accounts, but there are no journalists anywhere in the world — according to public opinion — who do the job better than our journalists.

Really? Let us persist with questions: Do journalists not have a point of view? Do journalists survey the whole world scape with precision and fairness? Are the United States' journalists less biased than journalists elsewhere?

Those questions knock on the gates of such a large institutional complex in the United States that the faint knocking is sometimes not heard well. But the questions must be asked, and they deserve answers far more definitive than a mere chapter of one book.

For my part, I shall deal quite modestly with the issue of journalistic responsibility by doing nothing more than illustrating that there is such a thing as a journalistic point of view. There is a point of view even in United States journalism whether we want to admit it or not.

The procedure for this chapter will be quite simple. I have selected a news event from Latin America having the potential for international coverage. Next, I have reviewed what the international press did with the event, and selected four samples of news stories to analyze in more detail. Those samples will be examined in this chapter.

A meeting was held in Havana, Cuba, during the final days of July and the beginning of August 1978. It was the eleventh such convention, but the first time any of the meetings had been held in the Western hemisphere. A huge crowd of people attended, some as visitors and many as delegates from 140-some countries.

What was the meeting? Why was it held? Who attended? What happened during the proceedings? Let us study these and other questions about the meeting itself. And then there are questions about the coverage: Who reported the meeting? Which items were thought worthy of mention in the reports? Were the writers objective in their reportage? If they revealed their opinions, through what kind of devices did they convey their evaluations? And more particularly, how did the United States press compare with the foreign press?

Let us proceed then to the four reports:

—A feature article from *Gramma*, the official organ of the Central Committee of the Communist Party of Cuba.
—A news article released by the news agency Prensa Latina (PL), to its numerous member subscribers throughout the world.
—A news feature printed in *Time* magazine.
—A news story released by the Associated Press, and printed (possibly with editorial changes) in *El Diario de Hoy*, a daily newspaper of El Salvador.

Beside each article, I have scribbled a number of comments. After each article, I discuss the journalistic treatment. Then, the chapter closes with a chart comparing the journalistic treatments in the four articles and a discussion of the implications of these findings.

Gramma

The *Gramma* news feature is the longest of the four, and even so is abridged in the translation. The newspaper, while not of high mechanical quality (smudgy pictures, uneven type), is probably one of the most widely circulated periodicals in Cuba. Some copies reach the United States.

The entire issue of August 6 was devoted to the meeting, except for an insert that spells out completely a new "Children and Youth Code." Besides this feature of the inaugural events are many photos, reprints of speeches, and lots of headline copy.

Gramma feature article, August
6, 1978

*Magnificent Inauguration of the
XI World Festival of Youth and
Students*

← beauty and grandeur
← focus on opening event

● Fidel presided over the beautiful ceremonies in Latinamerican Stadium

Cuban leaders
given primary atten-
tion

● Raúl opened the huge youth meeting

● Alain Greşh spoke on behalf of the International Planning Committee

• Unforgettable expressions of unity and friendship among delegates and the people who went out to greet them as they passed through Havana streets

a positive note: "unity and friendship" participation of the Cuban people

Extraordinarily beautiful were the opening activities of the 11th World Festival of Youth and Students, held Friday, July 28, in Latinamerican Stadium. Commander in Chief Fidel Castro, first secretary of the Central Committee of the Party and president of the Council of State and of the Government presided.

free with editorial judgments, none of which is negative

who? what? when? where? Mr. Castro is a part of first paragraph

It was an unforgettable occasion which had its culminating moment when Army General Raúl Castro, second secretary of our Communist Party, opened the 11th Festival on behalf of the National Planning Committee of Cuba.

"unforgettable" — note the adjectives

Cuba's own political leadership shown to be in big role

At 6:40 in the afternoon, long columns of delegates, after parading through the principal avenues of the capital, entered the gates of the stadium where they were awaited by a happy multitude of other delegations and invited guests.

a joyful mood

A few minutes earlier, dignitaries had made their entrance, including Fidel, Raúl, members of

again, symbols of Cuban government

the Politbureau and of the
Secretarist of the Party; Luis
Orlando Domínguez, member of
the Central Committee, first
secretary of the National
Committee of the Union of
Communist Youth and president
of the Cuban delegation; other
members of the Central
Committee; guests of honor; heads
of delegations; and members of the
diplomatic corps.

The stadium gleamed brightly
with the flags of the participating
nations, colored banners, flags of
the 11th Festival. Meanwhile the
scoreboard lighted up with the
words "Welcome, delegates."

As a preamble to what would turn
out to be a fiesta of color, rhythm,
and movement, thousands of
athletes broke onto the playing
field, carrying banners with the
colors of the flower of the festival.
They skillfully arranged
themselves into the shape of the
Festival symbol while the crowds
shouted, "Viva world youth!"
"Viva Cuba!"

Heralds of our Revolutionary
Armed Forces then presented the
call to attention while the "human
blackboard" (flash card section)
made up of more than 4,500
students presented the word

an international meeting, yet Fidel and Raul are elevated while political organizations are honored also

the setting?
--bright and cheery
--"the stadium gleamed"

-- color and pageantry
note the active, skillful role "of thousands" whose enthusiasm is finally focused on two things: world youth and Cuba

here and later, reference to military units
the human blackboard to be mentioned often

"Cuba" and in its center the flower of the 11th Festival.

again and again —
the word Cuba

A cavalry then entered the stadium to the tune of the Invader Hymn. The riders, who wore the glorious uniforms of the soldiers of our war of independence in the past century, carried the national emblems of Czechoslovakia, Hungary, the German Democratic Republic, Romania, Poland, the Soviet Union, Austria, Finland, Bulgaria, and Cuba, countries that have previously hosted the 11 festivals (the German Democratic Republic has hosted two). This brought to a close the first part of the program.

military unit, in
historical context

a naming of countries
as in a roll call
of honor

note the adjective
"glorious"

At the head of a parade was the marching band from the state of Mayor General, after which came the flag of the 11th Festival, borne by Cuban delegates and participants of the Permanent Commission of the International Planning Committee, and of the International youth and student organizations. They also carried flags of the 145 participating countries.

another military unit

Cuban delegates and
organization

flags are powerful sym-
bols, here mentioned
frequently

The German Democratic Republic, because of its having hosted the previous Festival, marched at the head of the delegations, who then followed in alphabetical order.

Anti-imperialistic Solidarity, Peace and Friendship.

Then began two hours filled with emotion, as the fine representatives of the democratic, progressive, and revolutionary youth of the world expressed their affirmations of anti-imperialistic solidarity, peace, and friendship.

Among the noteworthy examples of cordiality and respect expressed in unending acclamations and watchwords were those offered by the Soviet delegation which raised up its national emblem and a huge red flag on which was the picture of the great Lenin; by the delegation of the Popular Republic of Angola, of Chile, Ethiopia, Laos, Mozambique, Nicaragua, Palestine, Puerto Rico; and those of the peoples of the Sahara, Vietnam, and Cuba.

Also included in the parade were representatives from Afghanistan, South Africa . . . (and 116 other countries and places, each mentioned by name in alphabetical order).

The Cuban Delegation
The entrance into the stadium of the Cuban delegation (last in the parade by virtue of its being from the host country) had a reception truly "out of this world" while on

the festival theme mixes politics with social-spiritual values

labels: fine, democratic, progressive, revolutionary

festival theme restated

the setting was bright and cheery, the mood -- cordiality and respect

reference to an important ally

anothe roll call of honor

and Cuba

every country! does the naming alone bestow honor? probably, and it honors Cuba in their having come

explains why Cuba is last

note "out of this world"-- which suggests the loftiness of the honor to Cuba

the human blackboard appeared
pictures of Martí, Gómez, Maceo,
Mella, Camilo, and Che. At the
front of the Cuban delegation
came the national emblem, carried
by Teófilo Stevenson, two-time
Olympic champion and world
champion of boxing. Then
followed the flag of the 11th
Festival, of the UJC, and of the
student organizations.

mention of
- historical heroes
- national emblem
- current hero
- national organiza-
  tions

The march of the 26th of July and
the march of the Guerrilla
Movement were played as the
representatives of our country,
dressed in typical *guayaberas*
(decorated shirts) passed in front of
the tribunal. After the dancing of a
final "conga" the magnificent
parade was completed. Many
delegations distinguished
themselves in their original
initiatives, among which the
African countries attracted
attention with examples of their
respective cultures.

- national military
  music
- typical, national
  garb
- national dance

and yet another singling
out of delegates
and countries for
honor

This second part of the program
came to a close as the multitude
that packed the sports complex
shouted, "Fidel! Fidel!"

how does second part
close? "Fidel!
Fidel!"

The program continued as a
chorus of 2,000 voices presented
the National Anthem, while the
human blackboard showed the
Cuban flag.

2,000 honor Cuba
through anthem
and flag

Then followed the solemn delivery of the flag of the Festival to the host country. Eight Cuban youth received the flag from an equal number of youth from the Democratic Republic of Germany, and they proceeded to raise it up on a flagpole as the liberator army presented a reveille.

solemn? religious solemnity?

reference to Cuban youth

Another impressive moment occurred later when the distinguished athlete of the German Democratic Republic Renata Stecher gave a torch to two-time Olympic champion Alberto Juantorena who then lit the larger torch that burned throughout the 11th Festival. After receiving the torch from Stecher and another nine representatives of countries who had earlier hosted the festivals, Juantorena walked up the stairs to the larger torch amidst a jubilant ovation, while the blackboard showed "Cuba 78."

another military reference

athletics are incorporated into the making of political identity

a torch is a flaming light -- another provocative symbol

the blackboard honors not athletics but Cuba

Messages

Messages sent to the 11th Festival from distinguished personalities were then recognized; among them were messages from Leonid Brezhnev, Erich Honecker, Todor Yivkov, Gustav Husak, Edward Gierek, Janos Kadar, Yu. Tse-denbal, Pham Van Dong, and Mengistu Haile Mariam.

interesting to read the selection of those whose messages are newsworthy

Alain Gresh, coordinating
secretary of the International
Planning Committee, gave a
welcome to the delegates, after
which Army General Raúl Castro
spoke.

*The naming is crucial,
be it the naming of
certain countries
or the naming of
certain Cubans.*

Gymnastics Spectacular
After the playing field was cleared
of the delegates and flags, a
gymnastics spectacular took place,
on behalf of anti-imperialistic
unity, peace, and friendship, the
greatest such event ever carried
out in our country. Participants
included 10,000 gymnasts, 4,560
members of the human
blackboard, a choir of 2,000
voices, 500 musicians, 60
guitarists, and hundreds of
technicians and helpers.

*another notation of
festival theme*

*"the greatest..." is an
editorial judgment*

*Size : "in numbers
is much comfort"*

Conceived by the specialists at the
National Institute of Sports,
Physical Education and
Recreation, it consisted of a
prologue, three acts subdivided
into two scenes each, and a grand
finale. The human blackboard,
given a formidable task,
accompanied each act with 48
placard presentations, which
gained the admiration of the
audience.

*authorship? Cubans,
of course*

a brief objective note

*but followed soon by
a reporting of Cuban
skill ... applauded*

The prologue was presented by
1,200 members of children's
clubs—up to the age of 5—and
1,269 youth from military schools.

*in the paragraphs
that follow ...*

The little ones executed their
routines to the tunes of "Gramma,"
"I want to be an Athlete," and
"The song of the children."

The spectacular continued with
the scene entitled "The Same Sun
That Shines on Us," presented by
1,472 students from the schools of
children's clubs and from José
Marti school; the scene entitled
"In Unity is Victory," by 1,269
students from military schools;
"Peace," by 1,470 students from
Presidente Allende school: "The
Future is Peace," by 972
youngsters from athletic clubs;
"We Are Part of a big Human
Family," by 1,280 students from
Lenin vocational school; and
"Song of Friendship," after which
all of the gymnasts participated in
the finale.

. . . note the writers'
mention of
-- size of group
-- institutions
-- naming of songs
or poems

In each of the scenes . . . they
showed the determination, the
dedication, the legitimate
revolutionary satisfaction, and the
enthusiasm of our people in
receiving the representatives of
the revolutionary, democratic, and
progressive youth of the world
. . . .

evaluation in terms of
-- ideological solidarity
-- enthusiasm
-- Cuba's reception

The Hymn of Youth and a deluge
of fireworks, accompanied by a
dancing of a contagious "conga"
concluded the indelible night.

fireworks -- another
bright light
Conga -- something
Cuban and lively

"indelible"-- editorial judgment

After eleven o'clock, the 18,500 delegates to the 11th Festival left the stadium, knowing that the Cuban people made a reality of what they had said, "Youth of the world, Cuba is your home."

final paragraph focuses on Cuba and Cubans

—*Written by Juan Carlos Santos and Roberto Gilf.*

Discussion of Gramma

Gramma presented its detailed narrative of the opening Festival event in such a way that several distinct purposes seem to have given to the writers their point of view. First, there was the obvious intention of preserving a comprehensive account for the historical record. Many of the details, such as a listing of all of the nations, would otherwise have been unnecessary.

An equally important purpose, with more immediate political goals in mind, seems apparent—the reinforcing of Cuba's ideological identity in the minds of its populace. The writers said in effect, "Look, here is your Cuba today fully involved in an important occasion. We rank among the best. Our performance was great. Cuba is in good shape. Be proud of your country."

This political purpose became evident in the writers' frequent references to symbols of light and color, to athletic prowess, originality and skill; to traditional symbols of flags and emblems; to military organizations, heroes, songs, and battles; to honored government leaders; and to government agencies. The program, it seems to me, was a carefully orchestrated explosion of sights and sounds that elicited awe for one's own nation—orchestrated in much the same manner as the

1933 Nuremburg Convention was orchestrated. And the *Gramma* article served to capture that symbolic "load" in somewhat the same fashion as did the filmed documentary of Nuremberg, entitled *"Triumph of the Will."* The report, then, was an extension of the event itself. The writers' point of view came from *within* the event. They were participants, just as the gymnasts were participants.

The journalists were careful to name allies and friends in a variety of honorable roll calls, and to delineate Cuba's enemy (imperialism). And the writers found it desirable to mention over and over again the Cuban participation in leadership, parade, ceremony, placard team, gymnastics, and even in activities in the streets.

In contrast to some of the articles to be discussed later, this *Gramma* article did not devote itself to negative, desultory remarks of any type. The event, according to the account, was only "extraordinarily beautiful."

Prensa Latina

Prensa Latina (PL) is a news agency, or "wire service", located in Cuba. It functions there in much the same way as Tass in the Soviet Union, Reuters in Britain, Agence France Press, New China News Agency, or the Associated Press and United Press International in the United States. It collects and disseminates news to subscribing newspapers, magazines, radio, and TV stations.

Prensa Latina is a regional agency. Not many media persons in the United States subscribe to it. Its market likely consists mainly of Latin American and socialist countries.

I picked up the Prensa Latina release in Costa Rica, where only a few media (*Radio Monumental* and *Libertad*) receive PL. *Libertad* printed the release, and may have done some editing to it (which is permitted). *Libertad*, a weekly organ of the Communist Party, prints information and discussion of a partisan nature. During the weeks preceding and following the Cuban festival, it devoted many pages to the events and polemics.

Prensa Latina (PL) news release

Havana, August 1 (PL) The President of the Council of State, Fidel Castro, traveled around to various parts of this capital to meetings between the Cuban people and delegates to the 11th World Festival of Youth and Students.

who? Fidel Castro

what? visited parties

where? Havana suburbs

Context? 11th Festival

when? last night

Last night, all of the participants in this youth assembly attended "block parties" organized by the Committees for the Defense of the Revolution and the Federation of Cuban Women, two of the largest public organizations of the country.

as in <u>Gramma</u>, the naming of the organization is important

One thousand eight hundred fifty five committees from six Havana suburbs hosted these expressions of solidarity, which was billed on the program as "the people of Cuba receive in their own blocks the delegates to the 11th Festival."

size

purpose? show solidarity

One of the places visited by the leader of the Cuban revolution was

note the identification of Castro: leader of Cuban revolution

the area where Chilean delegates met with residents of barrio El Vedado.

The unexpected arrival of Fidel Castro to the centers of festivities was received with public jubilation and everyone shouted, "Viva Cuba" and "Viva the Festival."

One of the things that has aroused most interest among the foreign delegates to this youth forum is the partipation in person of the President of the Council of State in the numerous activities of the Festival.

In the city of Alamar, located about 15 kilometers east of Havana, the Soviet representatives shared hours of fun and solidarity with the Cubans.

In other sections of this locality were delegates of Bulgaria, Poland, Romania, the German Democratic Republic, Yugoslavia, Hungary and Czechoslovakia.

Representatives of Latin America and the Caribbean were concentrated, for the most part, in the area of El Vedado, singing and dancing Cuban "congas" and improvising dance retinues that wound through the streets of the capital until the early hours of the morning.

To which party would Castro go? Which visit would PL report? the visit to Chileans who at this time were in particular ideological struggle

the leader shown to be admired
the leader shown to be available

reference to an honored delegation. "fun and solidarity." see *Time* magazine account

and the naming of selected others. Who is not named?

note the mention of
-- Caribbean neighbors
-- Cuban focus
-- fun and celebration

Various delegates told the Prensa Latina that the most important and extraordinary aspect of these "block parties" was the opportunity of sharing directly with the people of Havana.

journalistic "objectivity" is retained by using testimonials to say what needs to be said

Written by Aurora Morera.

Discussion of Prensa Latina

Even though Prensa Latina functions as an independent news agency, its performance in this piece of journalism was similar to *Gramma's*. Like *Gramma*, Prensa Latina limited itself to one event. (Both agencies covered other events in other articles.) Like *Gramma*, Prensa Latina was an approving and even admiring agent. And like *Gramma* Prensa Latina gave Castro the stage center, reported on delegate approval of things Cuban, identified crucial Cuban friends and allies, emphasized solidarity of the participants, and refrained from any negative innuendos.

But Prensa Latina differed from *Gramma* in a number of ways. It did not try to be exhaustive in its report, but instead took samples here and there. The article was much shorter. Instead of putting itself into the event as a participant, Prensa Latina posed as "objective" onlooker by being careful to attribute any positive evaluations to other spokesmen, by using so-called disinterested descriptions, and by guarding against explicit editorial comment. But the reader could feel that the Prensa Latina wasn't neutral. It carried a friendly point of view—the reports of the popular leader, the mention of the mammoth organizations that planned the block parties, the reference to the theme of solidarity, the accounts of delegate-populace interaction, and the testimonials of appreciation.

Prensa Latina's point of view may be put into better perspective if one knows that *Newsweek* magazine reported that the Soviet delegation moved off alone into semi-isolation, and that *Time* magazine reported some disquiet among delegates toward the Soviet Union. That's not at all how Prensa Latina saw things. PL told only of "hours of fun and solidarity with the Cuban people" while *Gramma* reported that the Soviets had a particularly creative parade unit.

Time

Time, the weekly newsmagazine, enjoys a very wide circulation in the United States, and a huge international audience. The article which follows appeared in its Latin American edition.

Time has initiated and perfected a type of "committee journalism." Information is gathered from a large variety of sources—some of which information may be only incidentally related to the story at hand—and then a writer in the home offices "compiles" and "interprets" this information, hoping to present the facts in an interesting manner.

Its competition is not so much the news agency, but rather other weekly newsmagazines such as *Newsweek* and *U.S. News and World Report*. So its concern is not to get the latest scoop, but rather to get an interesting angle and to provide an adequate interpretation of events.

The article below included a mug shot of President Fidel Castro saluting. On the opposite page were five excellently reproduced color photographs of stadium events.

Fidel's Youth Jamboree

Flogging the CIA at a socialist show trial

The Czech girls sported distinctive red-and-white jumpers; the Poles, whose national colors the Czechs had appropriated, came decked out in red and khaki. There was color (and congestion) aplenty in Havana last week, as some 18,500 young leftists from 140 countries, attended by 1,500 journalists and 13,000 other visitors, crammed into the Cuban capital for the eleventh World Festival of Youth and Students. The eight-day, $60 million propaganda orgy is socialism's ideological equivalent of a global Scout jamboree. This year, as the festival was held for the first time in the Western Hemisphere,

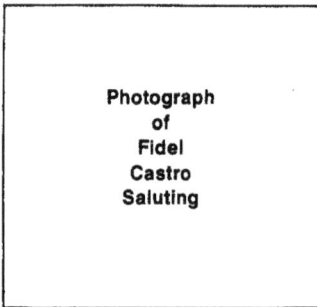

Photograph
of
Fidel
Castro
Saluting

Cuban President Fidel Castro. Hot air and narcolepsy.

friendly, informal style
a hint of delegate rivalry?

Color

"Congestion" implies a lack of planning or a surge of unruly participants

facts and figures

"crammed" implies unpleasant crowding

an extravagant expenditure

a partisan, political, propagandistic function

"orgy" hints at moral indiscretions

"Scout jamboree" -- patriotic kid stuff

"hot air" -- bag of wind

"narcolepsy" -- ?? sounds like degenerative mental illness! (see dictionary)

Cuban President Fidel Castro used the occasion to denounce, once more, the multifarious evils of U.S. "imperialism."

implies that Castro seized the event for personal and nationalistic purposes

Castro had spent two years planning the event, one of the few socialist spectaculars that offer the younger generation a good time. He also saw the festival as a good place to justify his country's

words and innuendos:
-- "multifarious" The adjective pokes fun at Cuba's perception
-- "imperialism" in quotes implies it really isn't imperialism

again note that Time sees the meeting as something concocted by Castro

-- extravagant expenditure of time

-- socialism is a drag

interventions in Africa. His policy needed a bit of bolstering, to be sure; at a nonaligned Foreign Ministers summit in Belgrade last week, some delegates attacked Moscow and Havana — rather than Western imperialism — as the current threat to Third World neutrality.

Time uses events in Europe to judge Castro and to demean the Festival

As Angolans, Russians, Mexicans, Britons, Vietnamese, and even a 400-member U.S. delegation trooped into Havana for singing, dancing, stadium pageantry, rap sessions and some frolicking on Cuba's beaches, they faced an additional event: the Youth Accuses Imperialism International Tribunal. A panel of eight "judges," headed by Uruguayan

Time's roll call includes the U.S.A.

fun: of four reports, only Time mentions beaches

here begins a long account of a trial

Physician Hugo Villar, heard scores of witnesses reel off accusations—some old, some true, many distorted or false—against the CIA. One star witness was Philip Agee, a former CIA agent now turned professional anti-agency muckraker. Other witnesses related details of a 1962 CIA poisoning scheme (during a time, admittedly, when the agency was indeed plotting to assassinate Castro), and of anti-Castro execution plots fomented as recently as 1976 in Mexico City. (The CIA calls the allegations of a Mexico City plot "absolutely untrue.") The main impact of these exposés on spectators was widespread narcolepsy; they were occasionally awakened by brisk applause from the army of Communist and Third World reporters covering the pseudo event.

At times, socialist solidarity wore a little thin. Castro himself delivered an early tongue-lashing of the communist Chinese, who had boycotted the festival. He castigated Peking for "insane political conduct," "repugnant betrayal of the cause of internationalism," and "perfidious, base arguments" against Cuba. The last, presumably, was a reference to

trial's judges in quotes

"reel off" implies a thoughtless listing

"some old, some true, many false"—a quick, easy editorial pass-off

Agee is labeled "muckraker"

an admission of guilt is quickly followed by a C.I.A. denial

evaluation of trial
-- narcolepsy, or sleepi-ness. the word sounds worse and thus is used to describe Castro in the picture caption
-- implication that only biased reporters (an army of propa-gandists) were interested

distractions from solidarity; Gramma and PL did not mention these

Peking's sharp denunciations of the Cuban military presence in Africa.

Other issues also threatened the mood of solidarity. Some British delegates wanted to question the 1,000 Russians attending the festival about Soviet human rights infringements; rather than cause an embarrassing fuss, they refrained. West German delegates split on the issue of how to deal with East Germany's imprisonment of Author Rudolf Behro.

Apart from the hot air, both political and real (Havana broiled under daily 90°F. temperatures), festival delegates seemed to get what they most wanted: some sightseeing and some fun. Reported *Time* Correspondent Richard Woodbury from the Cuban capital: "Flags and Christmas lights adorned the streets, and at night the broad Malecón, Havana's ocean-front drive, was festive with dancing. There were cultural and sporting events scheduled at almost every hour, from aquatic festivals to theatrical exhibitions to a Soviet-Cuban boxing match (the Cubans won). Restaurants were so crowded that they occasionally ran out of food, and there were a few other problems. Some members of

other problems:
British delegates vs Soviet delegates

West Germany vs East Germany

hot weather
(*Time* grudgingly admits delegates had a good time.)

note that the correspondent plays *Time*'s game. first, some light-hearted references to appearance of city, to the dancing, to the events, but turns negative over lack of food and, on next page, Cuba's unwillingness to accept credit cards.

the U.S. delegation, for example, naively assumed that Cuban restaurateurs accepted credit cards and traveler's checks. Not so; the American visitors were told to keep their capitalistic devices to themselves, that in communist Cuba the policy was cash only."

Does Time realize that its article reaches its climax over an issue of money?

Discussion of Time Magazine

Time's report was as anti-Festival as *Gramma's* report was pro-Festival. If *Gramma* was a happy participant, *Time* was a caustic critic. *Time* did not approve of Castro, passed off the Festival as a ". . . propaganda orgy . . ." and something akin to a ". . . Scout jamboree . . ." that produced ". . . hot air . . ." and ". . . narcolepsy. . . ." *Time* tried to establish that Castro usurped the Festival for political propaganda, that the CIA trials were a farce, and that the so-called solidarity of the socialist nations was indeed wearing quite thin.

Time used a large bag of journalistic tricks to good effect. Right off, the article was fun to read—easily the most interesting of the four reviewed in this chapter. Interest alone can give credibility. *Time* created interest through personalized accounts (the red-and-white jumpers of the Czech girls), crisp facts (18,500 participants, 140 countries, 1,500 journalists, 13,000 other visitors), curt judgments ("one of the few socialist spectaculars that offer the younger generation a good time"), the sneer ". . . hot air and narcolepsy . . .), on-the-scene reports, and odd happenings (restaurants running out of food, rejection of credit cards).

Time did not write about the ceremonies, the gymnastics spectacular (a boxing match was mentioned, and of course boxing is deemed more important in the United States than gymnastics), nor the interaction of delegates and the Cuban populace, nor the crowd's approval of Castro and the Festival. Among the events it chose to mention were the accusations against the CIA, the negative responses of U.S. delegates (*Newsweek* reported on the U.S. delegates too, emphasizing their membership in minority cultures, but reported on their approval of the Festival), and inter-delegate disquiet.

Unlike the other agencies who produced the articles in this chapter, *Time* attempted to look beyond Cuba to interpret the events of the Festival (the Belgrade conference, China's boycott, African military support, the CIA's response to the Mexico City "incidents") and took a wider sampling of Festival events (speeches, delegate feelings, the tribunal, street activities, and even restaurant supplies). But its selection missed what both *Gramma* and Prensa Latina focused upon.

Finally, *Time* refrained from mentioning anything positive about the ideological premises of socialism, or the results of socialism in Cuba, apart from the fact that the Festival was fun.

Associated Press, in *El Diario de Hoy*

The AP article came rather late, two weeks after the Festival. It is not known whether that delay was the doing of AP or the Salvadoran newspaper.

One must recognize that the Salvadoran government had just recently imposed what the *Miami Herald* said were the harshest repressive measures in Latin America against farmers and clergy who were agitating for social and economic reform. (The wealthy one percent of the agricultural population controls more than 40 percent of the arable land, whereas only 11 percent of the land is shared among the poorer 78 percent of the agricultural population.)

The article, appearing on page 6 of the August 13, 1978, paper, is sandwiched between two anti-terrorism articles.

El Diario de Hoy Sunday Aug 13

Cuban Children Swear Loyalty to the Soviet Union

Havana, Aug 12 (AP). A new child code has entered into effect in Cuba that urges all children to promise loyalty to the "anti-imperialist fight" and to "brotherhood and cooperation with the Soviet Union."

The new child and youth code was announced in a ceremony that took place at a "school for model children" in the presence of President Fidel Castro.

During the ceremony, two dozen children, dressed in the olive green uniforms of guerrillas, recreated the actual revolutionary attack by Castro in the Sierra Maestra mountains twenty years ago, advancing toward an armed fortress with toy machine guns. The only thing lacking were the beards.

note the headline's ideological tone

focus is on children (Festival is not mentioned.)

who? child code

what? now in effect

where? Cuba

note the two ideological labels

Castro is present at ceremony and, by implication, in the new code

report of ceremony focuses on military and revolutionary history . . .

and scoffs at beards while scorning the youngsters

Also in the classrooms

Thousands of children attended the ceremony. After the planning speeches, little girls took hands with the visitors and led them a short distance away where the theater groups and orchestras of the school demonstrated their arts.

objective report of events

Even though the activities were a part of a week of "anti-imperialistic solidarity," the United States and the Central Intelligence Agency were hardly mentioned.

a reference to Festival theme, without mention of Festival

that is, the U.S. and the C.I.A. were not mentioned at school.

Those in charge of writing the new child code, nevertheless, have assured that this theme will not be relegated to a secondary status in the classrooms.

but! U.S. and C.I.A. will be mentioned

The code orders that beginning now children be loyal to the "anti-imperialistic fight" and to relations of "brotherhood and cooperation with the Soviet Union and other socialistic countries."

return to code itself
-- restates opening paragraph
-- underscores ideological nature of code

This directive, contained in article two of section three of the code, is yet another evidence that the regimen wants to institutionalize anti-North American sentiments.

what is not mentioned --
-- code contains more than 100 articles
-- many of articles not ideological
-- concerns people to age 30
AP makes code into an anti-US document

Accounts of the activities of the CIA are as common here as the heroic feats of Jose Marti, apostle of Cuban independence.

return to CIA reference

Big Propaganda

The propaganda campaign has been more intense this past week than usual, owing to the presence of 20,000 leftist youths from all over the world who attended the 11th World Festival of Youth and Students.

> now a section on propaganda,
> set in context of a
> meeting of "leftists"
>
> the editors do not insert
> information about their
> own delegation to the
> Festival

A large number of Cubans and invited guests visited daily a new exhibition entitled "The CIA: Crime and Subversion."

> Suggestion that visitors,
> caught in lines, could
> not escape the voice
> of propaganda

The visitors who had to stand in line were shown documentaries against the CIA through two television sets installed at the entrance.

The regular programs on national television persist in the theme. This past week episodes relating to the invasion of the Bay of Pigs and other similar actions were replaced by sessions of an international tribunal, assembled to investigate the activities of the CIA.

> television is used by writer
> to indicate a subtle
> private enterprise
> bias
>
> -- doctrinaire programs
> -- no programs of en-
>   tertainment

Politics on TV

Of course, Cuban television does not offer programs for pure enjoyment. Apparently its concentration on themes of political propaganda doesn't allow sufficient time.

> the latter remark has
> a snide tone, similar
> to that earlier refer-
> ence to beards

Nor is the slightest expression of

ideological pluralism permitted. The children's code, for example, anticipates the "development and indoctrination" in "devotion to the cause of socialism and communism."

It orders, furthermore, that the "Communistic formation" of youth be a "high aspiration" of the state and similarly of the Cuban family.

The majority of the Cubans seem to accept this political reorientation toward the Soviet Union and its alienation from the United States, as if it were a perfectly reasonable response to what has happened in the past 19 years.

While the CIA, according to government statistics, has gotten involved in some 400 actions against the island, ranging from assassinations to acts of sabotage, the Soviets have helped Cuba maintain its economic development, which currently functions at a level ranging from one to three million dollars a day.

by this paragraph, the writer is not reporting an event or a week, but rather, interpreting the code and the political system that produced it

although the complete code concerns many aspects of growth, the writer fixes on the ideological

the writer even interprets the people's acceptance of the code by saying that 19 years of propaganda have led people to accept the Soviets and to condemn the U.S.A.

Discussion of AP and El Diario de Hoy

It is difficult to distinguish the news agency from the subscribing agency, in this case the Associated Press and the Salvadoran paper. The dynamics of wire-service journalism make the distinction difficult. The wire service

will likely carry many articles of one event. Associated
Press may have carried a score of Festival articles. Those
may have been written by full-time Associated Press
correspondents, part-time Associated Press "stringers,"
or by journalists working on AP-member newspapers,
whose stories were "picked up" by the wire and
distributed to the network. Any member paper, then,
may select from the daily offering, taking what it wants
and rejecting what it doesn't want. Further, it may
introduce editorial changes—deletions, modifications,
additions, a reordering of paragraphs, a rewriting of
headlines—according to liberal standards set up by the
wire service.

Without seeing the original release from AP, it is
impossible to establish who wrote what, how AP modified
it, and then how *El Diario* handled it. Certainly a process
of "gatekeeping" took place.

If *Gramma* was an approving participant, and Prensa
Latina a partisan onlooker, and *Time* a caustic critic, then
the "writer" of this article would be a sly political spook,
intending to frighten readers away from the evil clutches
of totalitarian socialism.

The key events of the Festival were not mentioned.
The Festival itself was mentioned incidentally, and with
the barest of facts. Salvador's own delegation was not even
announced.

Instead, the "writer" moved over to announce a new
youth code, and used that "occasion" to report upon and
discuss Cuba's program of ideological indoctrination.

The writer did not discuss the code in its fullness. (The
code happens to be a carefully planned, fully coordinated
expression of Cuba's highest hopes for all of its people
under the age of 30, and discusses guidelines in school

curriculum, arts, physical education, labor, values, political participation, and other areas. More than 100 "articles" review these guidelines.) Rather, the writer focused upon one article in the code that urges national loyalty and an identification with the philosophical, social, and economic character of socialism.

The lead paragraph concerned the code, and several subsequent paragraphs restated that lead paragraph, but much of the article pulled in information and impressions of yet other efforts to develop and indoctrinate the "children." On several occasions the writer sneered (the children who recreated a guerrilla battle scene didn't wear beards; Cubans don't have time to develop entertainment programs on television), but usually he followed the tenets of "objective" journalism—letting facts provide the evaluative load he wanted to deliver.

The writer, while reporting on certain activities in Cuba, seemed not to be as interested in an impartial reporting of news as in saying, "See what's going on in that socialist country! Beware lest you too be taken in by Castro and your children are forced to pledge their allegiance to a false god."

Meanwhile, El Salvador was repressing its population of impoverished *peones*.

Implications of This Study

Even journalists have points of view! In Havana, one journalist reported on the color, the pageantry, and the socialistic fervor displayed in opening night ceremonies. Another chose to report on President Castro's visits to block parties. A third opted to feature a new Cuban code rather than the Festival.

Those points of view are evident not only in what a

journalist chooses to write about, but also what he or she thinks of it all. One reporter said over and over that Cuba's participation was very good. Another revealed personal attitudes by emphasizing the interaction, the solidarity, and the fun. A third was a bit caustic, calling it a scout jamboree and a propaganda orgy, and focused upon the dissentions and logistical problems. A fourth was a confirmed antagonist, using the occasion for political card-stacking.

The four news reports we examined present four distinctively different images, as though the reporters had been at four different events. Had we included more samples from international reportage, we would have encountered even more diversity. The Soviet press, for example, focused upon the warm reception given to the letter of greeting from Leonid Brezhnev, read at the opening activities. *The Miami Herald* poked fun at the quick paint jobs in Havana—a bit of rouge on the face to seduce visitors.

A succinct comparison of the four news accounts is presented in the chart on pages 220-221.

I have made a case over the journalist's point of view primarily because people do not recognize that such a thing exists. As I indicated at the beginning of this chapter, we imagine professional journalists to be above bias. For many of us, the front page of the newspaper is to be read, not doubted. People believe in Walter Cronkite, they don't distrust him. Of course, errors in detail get into local news—it was a cousin instead of a sister, Smith instead of Smyth, 313 South Maple instead of 315 South Maple—but such errors don't really skew the overall picture. There is more complaining over the elimination of a comic strip than over the misreporting of news.

This type of uncritical consumption of news is a problem that compounds itself if readers always get all of their news from the same source. If a second or a third report from this same source reconfirms what was read in the first report, then the typical reader believes that truth will certainly have been established. It is an exceptional reader who will travel to the public library to find a half dozen accounts of a significant event, in hopes of getting the whole truth. Just as the reader on South Maple Street, Middle America, allows one source of information to feed his or her attitudes, so the uncritical readers of Salvador believe what the papers tell them.

So what? What does it matter if there is a journalistic point of view? After all, it was just a convention in Havana. There are a thousand events more important than a convention. And further, there will be no catastrophe, either in the United States or Salvador or in Russia, if a reporter doesn't get it all quite right. Aren't we making a mountain out of a molehill?

In my opinion, not at all. In the first place, the assembly in Cuba was important, for it gave revealing clues to understanding the development of socialism as well as comprehending what's going on with our next-door neighbor, Cuba. If all reportage of socialism is biased, how can we make intelligent policy decisions about it? If all reportage of Cuba is derogatory, how can we have correct information to feed our opinions?

Further, if journalistic points of view limit what we learn about a convention in Havana, how do journalistic points of view affect what we learn about Iranian revolutionary movements, China's political upheavals, continental shiftings in Africa, genocide in Cambodia, or refugees from Vietnam?

A Comparison of Four News Accounts About 11th Festival of Youth and Students

Cuba, July 29, 1978, and Following

	Gramma	Prensa Latina	Time	Associated Press
news peg	opening ceremonies	block parties	festival as whole	a new children's code
focus	color, pageantry, success of first night	Castro's visits to parties	an occasion for propaganda, a disparity between word and fact	children must promise loyalty to socialist regime
emphasis	Cuba's participation — very good	interaction, solidarity, and fun	jamboree, propaganda, dissentions, logistical problems	totalitarian's restrictive devices and propaganda strategies
role of Fidel Castro	presiding, crowd shouts, "Fidel! Fidel!"	unexpected visitor elicits jubilation and admiration	used occasion to denounce U.S., tongue-lash China, "hot air"	attended ceremony at school, his guerrilla heroics relived by students
U.S.	mentioned in list of 116 countries, listed alphabetically	not mentioned	mentions criticism of U.S. "imperialism," the CIA; reports size and complaints of U.S. delegation	interprets "attempts to institutionalize anti-North America sentiments," reports propaganda efforts against CIA

evaluative words	beautiful, unforgettable, skillful, happy, glorious, indelible	largest, jubilation, fun, important, and extraordinary	color, congestion, crammed, $60 million, propaganda orgy, hot air, narcolepsy, fun	code urges, orders propaganda campaign, development and indoctrination, political reorientation
problems	none	none	congestion, untruths, expensive, absence of solidarity, hot weather, rejection of credit cards	scoffs that child impersonators of guerrillas didn't have beards; Cuba doesn't have entertainment programs on TV; ideological pluralism not permitted
symbols of reference	among many: flags, battle hymns Lenin, Marti, Gomez, Maceo, Mella, Camila, Che, Guerrilla movement, guayabera	viva Cuba viva the Festival Fidel Castro the people of Cuba	Scout jamboree U.S. "imperialism" (in quotes)	
point of view	historian, admiring participant	reporter, approving onlooker	interpreter, critic, cynical scoffer	analyst, confirmed antagonist
prose style	flowery, subjective	professed "objectivity"	personalized journalism	professed "objectivity"

Information, as we pointed out early in the chapter, is the stuff that attitudes are made of. Attitudes, when they eventually express themselves, become opinions. Opinions, when they "move around" in the street, help to form public opinion. Public opinion generates public policy. Thus the route from information to public policy is very clear.

I believe strongly that U.S. policy toward Latin America has been shaped and reshaped by the information fed into the United States by ambassadors, by news agency correspondents, by public relations writers of multinational companies, and by tourists. Therefore it would be foolish for us to say that even one incomplete or unfair report of an event is inconsequential.

How fair is the United States press? I have always heard, even in graduate journalism classes, that American journalism was superior to any in the world. This impression is often reinforced when the American press tells us of the shenanigans of the foreign press. (For example, when more than a million Iranian people demonstrated for the removal of the Shah on Sunday, December 10, 1978, the U.S. press agencies did not hesitate to tell its readers that the Iranian offical press reported erroneously that the demonstrations were on behalf of world human rights.) But I do not know of any objective measurement of the international press that could deliver an authoritative valuation of the fairness of the U.S. journalistic product.

What I can report, however, is my own surprise as well as disillusionment when I lived long enough outside of the United States to hear foreigners bemoan the systematic prejudice of the "imperialist and capitalist" press of the United States. Those allegations of distortion rival any criticism I ever heard of the Communist propaganda machine.

Latin American critics tell us, for example, that we don't really know the true story of modern Cuba. The U.S. press misinformed the American public on the exploitative role of the U.S. sugar companies in pre-Castro Cuba, the U.S.-run brothels of Havana, the repressive regime of President Batista, the motivations and strategies of the Castro guerrillas, the nature of the socialist revolution, the reason for refugees fleeing to Miami, the justification for the expropriations of foreign industries, the rationale for prescribed food quotas, the story of the aborted Bay of Pigs invasion and other CIA attempts to overthrow Castro, the character of Cuba's alliance with the Soviet Union, and more recently Cuba's involvements in Africa. By repeating this long list of charges, I am not intending to side with Castro's socialist government. I am merely reporting that Latin Americans accuse us in the same measure that we accuse others.

After hearing such charges, I have given more attention to what the U.S. press indeed says about Castro. And I have found continuing attempts to depreciate Cuba and its leader. To illustrate, in the October 2, 1978, issue of *Time*, its popular "People" column featured Castro in Ethiopia, watching a parade. A prominent photo at the top of the page showed the president slouched in a chair, sleeping. By implication, Castro is an uncultured and unappreciative guest. The picture was kind of a joke, I suppose, excepting that it serves to reinforce the stereotype of Castro as an uncouth oddball from the mountains who destroyed free Cuba. One may find 18 years of such "loaded" reportage that focuses on his clothing, his beard, his cigar, the length of his speeches,

and recently the 2:00 a.m. timing of a press conference.
All the while, the more essential content of the Cuban
revolution, which apparently receives the overwhelming
support of a vast majority of Cubans, is not reported. In
keeping with this denigrading of Castro, *Time* in its
account of the Festival captioned Castro's photo, . . .
"Hot air and narcolepsy."

If I seem to be accusing *Time* magazine more than
others, it is only because *Time* does us the favor of
reporting *something*. Many other U.S. agencies don't
bother with Cuba.

I suspect that an impartial judge from Mars might say,
"Yes, U.S. journalism is bolstered by an elaborate
training program, a laudable credo, and superior
mechanical facilities, but these advantages cannot assure
reliable delivery of information." And I wouldn't be
surprised if the Martian would remind us that no
journalist is free from ideological commitments, nor free
from governmental and commercial pressures, nor from
social expectations, nor cultural conditioning, and—I can
hear the creature chuckling—no journalist is free from the
expectations imposed by the journalistic profession itself.

If we were big enough in spirit to look through this
larger perspective that the Martian has, we might not be
so arrogant about the rightness of our press, nor would we
so flippantly reject the suggestions that foreigners offer
us. Further we might let the foreign point of view
complement what we have learned from our own
journalists.

I do not wish to imply that point of view is inherently
evil, either in personal vision or in journalistic vision.
Point of view indicates the rich diversity of human
experience. But when a person allows himself to believe

that his field of vision is a complete vista of the world, he shall fall into prejudice. And worse, when a journalist would have us believe that one angle of one news event is the truth, the whole truth, and nothing but the truth, we allow ourselves to be deceived.

Is it too much to hope that the North American press include Latin America more regularly in its world scape, and that its best journalists survey that world scape with precision and report to us more fairly what they see? We need that kind of information.

And All These Things

*Notes on materialism and the accumulation of
possessions in a country that has (the United States) and
a continental region that wants (Latin America)*

During my family's first Christmas abroad, we answered a knock at the door. A humble peasant woman, whose Spanish we could not understand very well, introduced herself as the wife of a workman we learned to know. She had come to bring us dark banana leaves in which were wrapped what looked like pasty cornmeal patties: We invited her into our house, and a few minutes of strained conversation followed. Her child, who wore only a shirt, stood timidly by her side until he squatted and made a bowel movement upon the floor. The woman did not seem upset with the child, but after several more minutes of simple Christmas-talk, she and her child left.

Our family has often recalled that event. After falling in love with Latin American peoples and their culture, we feel ashamed now about that visit, for we were totally unprepared to accept her lovely Christmas gift of *tamales* and friendship.

My perception of those "pasty cornmeal patties" was so different from hers that we could not really share the true spirit of the season. To me, they were something wrapped in dirty leaves, something prepared in an unsanitary kitchen, something made with pork that might have trichinosis, something made by a woman whose child habitually dirtied the floor. To her, the *tamal* was a beautiful cultural tradition: everyone ate *tamales* on Christmas eve. (And yes, a *tamal* must be wrapped and boiled in banana leaves to provide the correct flavor.)

Tamales "and all these things" have something to do with culture. Edward T. Hall has written:

> Materials and the rest of culture are intimately entwined. . . . Men and women dress differently, tools go with work, time and space are measured with instruments, there are toys for play, books for learning, and even material signs of status. The relationship between materials and language is particularly close. Not only does each material thing have a name, but language and materials are often handled by man in much the same way. It is impossible to think of culture without language or materials.[1]

In this final chapter we shall explore how the relationship of culture and materials might cause two people to see the same thing from two different points of view. I shall close the chapter by examining how today's cross-cultural communication is made up largely of a commerce of *things*, or said in other words, messages that are materialistically motivated.

Culture, Things, and People
"Material and the rest of culture," to repeat Hall's words, "are intimately entwined." How precisely does that "entwining" take place?

Linguists such as the late Benjamin Whorf have asked
that question, but there has never been a definitive
scientific answer to satisfy cultural scholars. Lacking such
proof, we are permitted to speculate on an answer. If
materials and the rest of culture are intimately intercon-
nected, then it might follow that the peoples of one
distinct culture would perceive, label, and use material
objects differently from the peoples of a different culture.
One might suggest, for example, that the middle-class
North American culture represents a common understanding about certain *things* that might not be similarly
held by a certain class of Latin American peoples.

Let us consider the material object known as *carpet*. To
the Wisconsin housewife, carpet is likely to mean a woven
fabric of dyed wool, cotton, or synthetic fiber, used as a
floor covering. Usually it is laid upon a rubber mat to
assure longer service. The carpet is swept several times a
week, preferably by a vacuum sweeper that has a beater
bar to loosen the sand and dirt particles which can cut the
fibers. Once a year, the carpet is shampooed with a
nondetergent cleaner. A good carpet, which can be
purchased and laid for $15 a square yard, can add elegance
as well as warmth to the home.

To understand how much that definition of *carpet* is
culturally influenced, one must recognize that floors and
carpets are very much a part of the Wisconsin culture.
There, people sit on carpet in front of the fireplace, they
play Monopoly on carpet, they walk stocking-footed on
carpet, and use up Saturdays by pushing the Hoover over
carpet. If a baby throws up on the carpet, they know to use
a damp cloth quickly, so that no stain will remain. Animal
urine is more difficult to extract from carpet, but there are
chemical compounds mixed with sawdust that can be

spread onto such deposits. Take a look at house and home magazine ads for a depiction of the ever-present carpet.

To a lower-class Latin American *señora*, carpet is a ridiculous idea. The best floor is wood that can be waxed and polished. The most practical is tile, which the maid can mop daily. To this *señora*, the floor of the house is an extension of the floor of the tropical earth. One doesn't set purses or briefcases onto the dirty floor. One doesn't walk barefooted or stocking-footed on the floor. One doesn't put shoes, which have just touched the floor, onto a chair. Only the best housewife can keep her floors clean. Carpet? Imagine the dirt that collects in the carpet! Imagine the mold that rainy season would bring! Imagine how many years one would have to work to cover a floor with carpet, and then more years to buy a sweeper! And this all assumes the use of electricity. No, carpet is good only for the very rich who want to show off their wealth.

The thought patterns as well as the emotional responses to the material object *carpet* grow out of a person's experience with floors. That experience is likely to be *similar* to the experience of neighbors, but possibly *dissimilar* to the experience of peoples of another culture. Said in another way, a culture exercises its uniqueness in many ways, even in the giving of its own meanings to something like carpet.

It is my hunch that how one sees a thing is consistently influenced by one's culture. It would not surprise me to discover that a Hoosier teenager (a) and a Guanacaste teenager (b) would think differently of these five items:

1. *A 1967 Toyota*
   a. A 12-year-old, worn out and rusted import.
   b. A $4,000 status symbol, waxed monthly, polished daily, and parked in a locked garage.

2. *Street Cleaner*
   a. A $30,000 Elgin vacuum machine, with two-ton dust bin and hydraulic dump, that traverses all city streets once weekly to pick up soot, sand, and loose stones.
   b. A *peon*, bottom of the employment ladder, who sweeps the *barrio* gutters once weekly, picks up paper and refuse, carries the litter in a broken wheelbarrow to the ravine, and dumps it there.

3. *Miracle*
   a. A supernatural happing; such "events" went out of style when people started keeping scientific records.
   b. A blessing, such as a gift of healing, given by the Virgin.

4. *Godfather*
   a. A movie of crime and violence, starring Marlon Brando and grossing more than $100 million.
   b. A person, selected by one's parents, to whom one can turn in time of need.

5. *McDonald's*
   a. The cheapie, fast-food hamburger chain with the golden arches.
   b. A foreign-owned and expensive restaurant in San Jose where you stand in line to order the *hamburguesa con queso*, which they put on a tray; you then carry it to a table and eat it there.

Although the "definitions" shown above may miss the mark somewhat, I am convinced that things, as they appear to the typical Hoosier, may not always thus appear to the Guanacastecan. In other words, a spade is a spade . . . if you see the spade from my angle. A rose is a rose . . . maybe.

If such differences of perception of a *carpet* or a *car* or a *hamburger* affected only our fleeting impressions, then we might settle for writing an essay showing the interesting differences of culture, and nothing more. But I believe that culture's influence goes far deeper than superficial impressions. Culture affixes values to objects. That is, in the process of suggesting the "meaning" of an object, culture attaches a kind of a price tag to material goods. This price tag indicates something of the esteem that members of the culture *ought to have* toward the material object.

A sweat shirt with a North American university logo is priced at maybe $5.95 in the campus bookstore. Students wear them, but don't make too much fuss about them. Some students might even sneer about the not-so-subtle device of university promotion. In Latin America, those same sweat shirts are probably valued far more highly than on their original university campus. For one thing, sweat shirts of that quality fabric and construction cost up to three times as much as in the United States. In addition, the sweat shirt has add-on value: the prestige of having studied in the States, or at least being associated with an established North American university.

The value is more than its monetary worth. The value has to do with a more inclusive system of valuation, that reaches beyond the purse to the brain and the heart. Why do people buy what their neighbors buy? Why do they use products in the way their neighbors use products? The answer to those questions has to do with the internalization of values which become influences of primary force. When indoor plumbing becomes the mode, outdoor toilets become a joke. But more than a joke. Indoor plumbing can bring with it a solid value strong enough to exert pressures such as disapproval or even rejection of those who refuse to destroy their outhouses and install indoor bathrooms.

In arriving at object values, the people of a culture tend to put the price tag not only upon the object itself, but also upon the people who "possess" the object. In other words, the object-value and the person-value become confused. A person is inclined to estimate the value of another person in terms of the material objects he possesses, rather than in terms of the spirit that enervates him. Who rents his house? Who owns his house? Who drives a Ford? Who drives a Lincoln?

If a culture in fact defines and affixes values, which in turn mold the reputations of its members, it should be evident that a member of one culture would find it difficult to intercept the object-values and the person-values of a culture different from his own. To be specific, the typical rural midwestern North American will have had such an association with material possessions that he will not be able to understand the use of material by, let us say, a very poor Costa Rican. Why? Because his association with material objects in Illinois will have affected his own value systems, both as those values pertain to material objects and to people.

To put that general assertion into understandable and human terms, let us consider a "person" from downstate Illinois whose profile will be a composite of impressions of various midwesterners. She is not a real person, nor shall we allow her to represent all midwesterners. We'll simply call her a member of that culture, and give her the name "Gladys." As you read, be mildly aware of the words that are listed in the column to the left; we shall return to them.

Selected Words	*Gladys*
Christmas	Christmases past always made Gladys feel

store
toy
music
rain

food

excited, like a little child. But today in the Klinestown Mall, the toys looked flimsier than they did on TV. "Rudolph the Red-Nosed Reindeer" seemed out of place, what with the sloppy rain outside. And Gladys was mad at herself; she had vowed to lose weight, but when she had passed the soda fountain, she bought a tasteless sundae.

water
bag
gift

post office
bread
telephone
electricity

Even though she hurried to the car, the rains made her shopping bag plenty wet, but she hoped none of the gifts would be damaged. She slipped into her station wagon, eased out of the parking lot, and headed downtown, for she wanted to mail the Christmas cards at the post office, buy fresh bread, cash a check, and pay the phone and electric bills at the drive-in window.

family
fear

zone
politician
prices
church

Christmas this year seemed only to signal that time was passing. Now that her family was about grown, did she have a fear of aging? A suspicion that she and Milton had little in common, apart from the children? (On Monday nights, why couldn't she share a bit of the hoopla when the Lions moved the football into the end zone? Why couldn't he talk politics or prices with her? Why couldn't they attend a Christmas party or at least go to a music program at church?)

newspaper
police
robber

school
alcohol

Her moodiness made her feel guilty. Maybe she should take Pastor Wallace's advice, "read the police news, the accidents, the fires, the robberies, then you'll know how good you have it." Probably right. Bill her son was a mess in high school—a drinker, a nuisance at home, always arguing with his "old man"— and yet here he was now married to a decent

girl
baby

fun
car
movie
Coca-Cola

soccer
summer

girl and proud papa of a baby boy. Susan, her older daughter—say what you want about her personality—she still had good sense. Her definition of fun was not hot-rodding around at night with guys, but going to a movie, then returning for homemade pizza, Cokes, and records (which Milton always said were too loud). And anyone would be proud of tomboy Nelly, best soccer player of Mayflower, holder of a water safety license, and summer camp counselor.

uncle
heart attack
work

The girls knew their mother was depressed, so they urged her to get a job, and at the same time told their Uncle Clarence, whose heart attack had slowed him down, to give her work at his home furnishings store. She accepted the offer, but not until the new year would she begin.

money
social security
tax

She agreed to work for the girls' sake, not for the money. After all, she'd bring home maybe $150 a week, after social security and tax deductions. No, the money wouldn't make her rich.

interest
house
tool

chance
garbage
dish
decoration
bathroom
clothing
doctor

What would she do with it? Was she to be blamed for having no interest in paying off the house mortgage? Wasn't that Milton's respon-sibility? When he wanted a tool for his shop, he got it with hardly a second thought. She now had a chance to even things out but she honestly couldn't think of what to buy. A garbage disposal? A dishwasher? Redecorate the upstairs bathroom? Get some good clothing? She had read about cosmetic surgery, but wondered how a person would explain that to a doctor, or to a husband.

chance

The rain seemed to fall even heavier, so she turned the wipers to high. To counter the monotonous beating, she pushed the ON button in time to hear, "Rapidly falling temperatures, freezing tonight, and 90 percent chance of measurable snowfall tomorrow." When Dean Martin started singing "I'm dreaming of a white Christmas," Gladys involuntarily hummed along, and soon began to feel like a child.

This profile, as we indicated before, is a composite of impressions that reveal neither a saint nor a despicable character, but rather a person somewhat like the rest of us who is a product of her culture. We have feelings about rain, about Christmas, and about growing older.

Now, let us make another profile, this one of an extremely poor Costa Rican man, again neither a saint nor a despicable character, but a product nonetheless of a culture. As in the previous profile, selected nouns will be woven into the profile.

Selected Words

Chepe

bag
bread
Coca-Cola
newspaper
work

In the early morning hours Chepe slinks hesitatingly through the *barrio*, walking a bit sideways, with one hand timidly covering his face, the other clutching his paper bag in which he always carries bread and a Coca-Cola bottle filled with coffee, and his *machete* wrapped in newspaper. His eyes search left and right, looking for work, testing the day's prospects, for Chepe is the *barrio* grass and weed cutter.

clothing

garbage

He always wears the same clothing—a dull brown shirt that hints of earlier stripes, baggy pants that have been picked out of a garbage box. His feet are flat and leathery, his hands permanently stained green. His eyes are bloodshot, his teeth darkened by decay.

car
money

He comes from "La Jungla," a large shack town that lines both sides of the ravine south of the city. He's never ridden a car, and seldom a bus, for on really good days he earns only $4. Usually it's far less, so he can't affort 15-cent rides.

family
house

bathroom

decoration

At home are his common-law wife and seven children, who live in a 12 X 8 section of a confusion of cardboard and corrugated tin *casuchas*. When they're all at home, they can't sleep in the room, not even if one sleeps on top of the table, and one under it. They share a toilet with eight other families, although it's hard to keep just anyone from using it. The nicest part of the house is a poster Chepe found on the street of a young colt running over a meadow.

water

police

electricity

robbers

As others will tell you, life is hard in "La Jungla." The water pipes that the city laid to the area are broken at so many places that residents have to carry water daily, and it's not uncommon for the *barrio* to be out of water for two weeks at a time. Once they tried to protest by throwing limbs across a road, but police brought a bulldozer to push the materials away. Since there is no electricity, families rely on candles, or better, they go to bed at dark. But in the night, robbers rove the little alleys, unmolested by the police who stay clear of "La Jungla" unless there is a violent crime.

Chepe feels lucky in one thing: "La Jungla"

politicians

tax
fear

has not been condemned by politicians who, to attract the vote of the rich people, burn down poor slums. Chepe knows of other people who've been driven from home after home, and sometimes forced to live in government houses built by tax money. How terrible to return at evening to a mound of ashes! Yes, there is a kind of permanence at "La Jungla."

school
toy
dish

girl

baby
food

Beside that bit of luck, there is mainly grimness to Chepe's life. Secretly he is ashamed of what he has given his children. Instead of attending school, his boys roam, sometimes playing with their bicycle rim which they guide with a stick; instead of eating from dishes, they use only the *tortilla*. Already he suspects that his daughters, like the daughters of his neighbors, will earn money for pretty clothing by sleeping with men. And then there will be babies, and he will have more mouths to feed.

store
prices

summer
rain

Christmas

doctor

His own woman demands far more money than he can supply. She says that the grocer always raises prices for rice and beans and milk. She is right. When was the last time he ate a piece of meat? Things are bad enough in the winter, but in the summer when there is no rain, the grass grows more slowly and Chepe has less work. Unfortunately in December, just the week before Christmas, he got a thorn in his foot, between the toes. The witch doctor in "La Jungla" could not take away the infection. When he could no longer walk, he hobbled to the public clinic where, after everyone else was waited on, a nurse kindly incised the wound and gave him

social security

uncle
interest

medicines. (Since Chepe has no formal employment, no person pays his social security, so he is technically ineligible for free medical service.) The loss of a week of work will cause hunger. He may have to beg *tio* Pepe for a loan, but till he pays the interest, the amount to return *tio* will be double the original amount.

fun

alcohol
soccer
movie
music
zone

telephone

church

chance
post office

Although daily life is cruel, Chepe lives for the possibility of a bit of fun on weekends. If he can hide money from his woman, he buys a pint of contraband *guaro*. But usually he is content to walk to town, watch a soccer game, look at the promotional photographs in the movie theater, listen to the weekly serenade in the park, and browse the American zone in hopes of finding a usable discard. (He once found a number of 25-*centimo* coins in a pay phone there.) He goes to weekly mass, not inside the church, but standing by the back door. He believes it might bring him luck, even though none of the lottery tickets he has bought from the sellers by the post office ever returned him a *centimo*.

heart attack

gift

Chepe slinks through the *barrio*. At mid-morning he learns that a man whose lawn he regularly cut has suffered a heart attack. That made Chepe sad, so he walks to the other end of the *barrio* to another of his "clients" whose garden is very large, and there cuts some lettuce and coriander, and carries them to the sick man as a gift. Chepe feels pleased and hopes the man is pleased.

Now that we have two "people" in mind, one from Illinois and one from Costa Rica, let us examine how some of the individual words, listed in the column on the left,fitted into the profile.

Baby
—a result of prostitution; another mouth to feed (Chepe).
—evidence of stability, maturity of son (Gladys).
Bathroom
—a toilet shared by eight families (Chepe).
—something to redecorate (Gladys).
Car
—a vehicle he has never ridden in (Chepe).
—the vehicles of youthful carousing at night (Gladys).
Dish
—a *tortilla* (Chepe).
—something to be washed in a machine (Gladys).
Garbage
—source of a pair of pants (Chepe).
—something that an electric machine can dispose of (Gladys).
Interest
—the doubling of borrowed money (Chepe).
—lack of desire (Gladys).
Newspaper
— a wrapper for a *machete* (Chepe).
— a possible source of bad news (Gladys).

These comparisions are "forced" in that they do not rise out of documented cases. However, each of the definitions fits comfortably into the profiles. And therein we find informal evidence that Gladys and Chepe, no matter how much they might wish to understand each other, would actually have very little common experience to build upon. The material things common to Chepe are not perceived, labeled, or used in the same way by Gladys.

The students in our college program in Central
America come from Gladys' culture, so they struggle to
understand people like Chepe. They try to comprehend
the horrors of life in densely populated shack towns. They
ponder, "How shall we best respond to the cripple who
asks us for a nickel?" One such student, Galen Martin,
wrote about different definitions of *box:*

> When I was young,
> people would abandon pets
>   in a lined cardboard
>   box,
>   along a country road.
> And we thought it very cruel
> And we felt pity for the
>   animals.
>
> This morning a family slept on
> a sidewalk in San José
> and the lady was
>   sleeping in a
>   box. [2]

It is not just the naive student from North America who
finds poverty incomprehensible. Denis Goulet has
written about this dilemma as it affects scholars and
experts:

> Chronic poverty is a cruel kind of hell; and one cannot
> understand how cruel that hell is merely by gazing upon
> poverty as an object. . . . The dominant emotions of a
> development scholar, a technical expert, or an educator are
> totally opposed to those of his "subjects." They are fragile, he
> is strong; he has knowledge, but they are ignorant. He
> understands how decisions are made, while they suffer the
> consequences of decisions they have not reached. [3]

Most midwesterners have never seen impoverishment; what problems they have seen "on the other side of the tracks" they subconsciously attribute to laziness, carelessness, or dissipation . . . something that a bit of hard work and a dose of religion would surely eradicate. No wonder that people who have never needed to pray, "Give us this day our daily bread," should feel a confusion of emotions when, in a touristy restaurant at ten o'clock on a chilly night, two thin, scruffy, ill-clad youngsters edge to the table and, obviously undernourished and hungry, ask for a piece of bread.

By this time, the reader may reply, "A bit unfair! You've compared a middle-class person from affluent United States with a lower-class person from underdeveloped Central America." True, but the same lack of coincidence in defining and using material things may be found when comparing any two cultures, even the rural American culture with the urban American culture north of the border.

Let us consider, for example, a person quite different from Chepe, but nonetheless from Central America—a very rich person. I make this particular choice because the "Gladys" that I have known finds the very rich more difficult to relate to than the very poor. The rural, midwestern North American has likely been schooled in the democratic and egalitarian tradition, conditioned by taboos against social discrimination, accustomed to the inquiries into the ethics of business and political leaders, limited by laws that rather effectively curb profiteering, and accustomed to the privileges of culture . . . at least as far as the regional midwestern community defines such things. She therefore has no backlog of experience with which to understand. . . .

—the prestige of traditional upper-class status.
—the unquestioned authority of the strong man.
—the privilege that comes with class.
—the conspicuous consumption expected of the rich.
—the formal courtesies used by the rich.
—the disdain of the *peon* expressed by the rich.

To see this nonalignment of cultures, let us build a composite of a youth from a very wealthy family who lives in Los Yoses of San Jose. We shall incorporate those selected nouns.

Selected Words	*Ricardo*
summer	On an early summer evening, 17-year-old
car	Ricardo throws himself into his Thunderbird (one of five in San Jose) and lays six feet of rubber en route to "the ledge," an empty lot overlooking Los Yoses, where his peers meet almost daily. Nobody knows quite when, why, or how the tradition got started, spending an hour or two on 17th street, across from the Quiros mansion (he is head of the supreme
newspaper	court), a half block from the newspaper
uncle	publisher, and one lot from his uncle's house
politician	(he is president of the legislative assembly). The younger teenagers, in imitation of their elders, congregate at the bottom of the hill,
toy	but since they don't drive cars, they bring their ten-speeds.

These gatherings are an escape for Ricardo. It happens that he flunked chemistry, and since his father couldn't get the grade changed, he has hounded Ricardo unmercifully to pass the re-exam, for he fully expects Ricardo to enroll

school   at the University of Michigan in September. (His grandfather got his degree there, and says he'll pay for Ricardo's education, but only if he goes to the University of Michigan.)

gift

tool

soccer

Ricardo's father promised a gift—a motivational tool: pass chem and you can go to the Daytona 500. Ricardo indeed wants to go, remembering the month-long drama of the world cup finals in Argentina (a gift for passing the re-exam in physics the previous year).

To tell the truth, Ricardo is ambivalent about the University of Michigan, but who is going to oppose a rich grandfather—a 10,000-acre cattle *finca* in Guanacaste, a dairy by Irazu, the horses he shows off in every parade, the

clothing

music

Coca-Cola

clothing store, the radio station and the record company in collusion, the Coca-Cola distributorship, the directorships, the foreign investments? . . .

family

rich

Ricardo pulls his Thunderbird to the curb (his family has seven cars, the nicest being a 1948 Roadster which his father won't let him drive), and nods a carefully constructed nonchalant greeting to the gang. He is among the richest, so he tries to pretend it isn't true. He comes regularly to the ledge, yet deep inside he is always self-conscious, not so much about himself but about his family.

dish

movie

doctor

His mother, for instance, is an embarrassment, a hopeless bore. Her idea of pleasure is a catered meal at the club, on dishes rented from England, a combo of old men in tuxedos playing waltzes, a 1950s movie, and an evening of alcohol. His dislike for his mother is the strongest emotion he has felt lately. She is, one might say, a commuter. She commutes to her Houston doctor for back treatments, and already knows which specialist will treat

heart attack	her husband when he suffers his heart attack. She commutes to Miami, not only for
Christmas post office	Christmas shopping, but for everything— maybe even to deliver some mail. She cannot remain where there is no commotion. With such a mother, how could Ricardo ever take a girl friend to his house?
girl clothing electricity fear	He is supposed to be able to look at one of the girls—in the opened drapes of today's chic—and feel electricity, but he feels only numbness, or is it fear?
social security car phone baby robber zone tax	Ricardo, for his own social security, stays in his car, but the others soon gather by him (he knows it is the money). Pablo asks to use Ricardo's car phone, and in a merciless prank, calls Santa Teresita church to ask which Sunday in May is best for a wedding for Diana. (Is she really pregnant?) Some of the kids are vile. Katya has already had an abortion. Carlos has been caught twice in thefts, yet some of the youth act as though they live in a special zone of immorality that will later allow them to avoid paying import taxes on their Mercedes Benz.
bread bag garbage	No one says it but everyone knows the ritual at the ledge: each person tries to do something "unrich" without being philistine. Ostentatious deflation. It is hard to match yesterday's feat. Today Susana casually lifts out a loaf of bread from an expensive shopping bag, and passes around a last supper, throwing the paper wrappers onto a heap of garbage that the gutter cleaner will pick up. Nothing more happens. Ricardo almost admires Susana and wishes she'd like him even without the Thunderbird.

house

food

rain

Dusk brings an end to the non-event, so
Ricardo drives home with his unknown
purposes unfulfilled. The house is empty
excepting for one of the maids who puts out his
supper. He doesn't care to eat what she made,
so he goes to his room, throws himself across
his bed and wonders how soon the rains will
come.

The reader will correctly have concluded that Ricardo's
culture is as foreign to Chepe as it is to Gladys. To Chepe,
Coca-Cola was a bottle for holding coffee. To Gladys, it
was a snack. To Ricardo, it was a profit-making company.
When Ricardo thought about *electricity*, it had to do with
sexual feelings rather than power lines that did not go into
Chepe's *barrio*. Gladys knew about the end *zone* of a
football field; Chepe knew about the American *zone* of the
city; Ricardo's friends imagined a territory of immunity
from law.

The point of this exercise is not to propose that culture
sits like a king on a throne, arbitrarily shaping the
meaning of words to his pleasure. No, culture doesn't
work that way. Rather, culture, which makes up the total
circumstances of a people's corporate life, becomes
something like the makers of a theatrical set, providing an
environment in which words can become dynamic.
Summer has special meaning for Chepe because his
livelihood depends upon cutting grass. Because Gladys
doesn't cut grass, her word *summer* yields to a different
dynamic—the development of her daughter Nelly who
swims and directs camping activities. Ricardo is at a place
different from either: *summer* is boredom, indecision, the
time to pass chemistry. And so one could go on and on,
showing the stage props and the unfolding drama.

The reader may persist in studying the middle-class person of Central America, and ask, "Because the middlers are neither very rich nor very poor, don't they share many of Gladys' values?"

If I may appeal again to the experience of our students' interactions with host families in Costa Rica, I would have to say that the fundamental differences between the middle classes of rural North America and of the Latin America I have known are so great that it is precisely in this economic level where most of our misunderstandings take place.

The making of the Latin American middle class does not necessarily parallel the making of the North American middle class. The latter is centuries old; the former is relatively new. It is likely that Latin America's middle-class person is not descended from an elite family, but rather ascended from a non-elite rural sector. Recently, many thousands of people have migrated from country to city in search of middle-class status.

The city has, as we know, been cruel to such people, sentencing them to the cardboard slums that surround large Latin American cities. But urbanization, industrialization, modernization have produced a middle class.

There has been a monetary impulse to the making of that class. This is not to claim that the Latin American middle-class is more money hungry than the North American middle-class. Rather, money is for them a new and totally significant thing. One must recognize that they come from rural areas where a money economy had not been highly significant. People worked for room and board. Gardens supplied food. Other essentials were obtained by trade. Then, with the coming of the transistor radio, people learned of material objects they might one day possess—if only they had money to make the purchase. They didn't want money in order to accumulate it, but to buy the products that radio told them about. In North America, on the other hand, the motivating forces propelling the middle class are many. Money is a crucial part of the whole, but not the whole. When one speaks of American middle-class life, it has to do with salary and K-Mart, yes, but also with association patterns, zoning, educational norms, security, mobility, and independence.

While both the North American and the Latin American middle classes are high-consumer sectors of their respective economies, there are crucial differences in type of goods consumed. For one thing, the Latin Americans have less money to spend. Their income is considerably less than the North Americans'. Second, the Latin American typically does not know the tradition of saving, so the wage earner is likely to spend his money as it is earned. Having little, therefore, he or she is likely to purchase what, in the eyes of the North American, is of minimal economic worth. Third, because the production and distribution pattern in Latin America lags behind that of North America, the things that Latins "go crazy over" are somewhat *passe* to North Americans who finished that fad months or years ago. And fourth, the aesthetic preferences of Latin Americans tend to reflect their more colorful, emotional, impulsive, expressive manner of being, while the North Americans tilt toward the more functional and sober northern Europe traditions. Hence, their respective purchases may differ.

There would be yet other ways to contrast the middle classes of North and South. The North's tradition of philanthropy, the South's more privatized spending; the

North's concern for the public sector, the South's
orientation toward the private sector; the North's peer
orientation to style of living, the South's family orientation, and so on.

I am not wishing to make value judgments on either
grouping. Indeed, if one wanted to evaluate the North
American middle-class culture, one could find many
ready critics in Latin America. Many people find the
social context for middle-class North American life not
altogether to their liking. When they visit the United
States, they speak admiringly of the cleanliness and
order, but they also note individual alienation, interpersonal distance, mechanistic procedures, crime and
violence, casual and even flippant disregard for tradition,
mobility that disregards home and family, extravagant
consumption of scarce natural resources, and a pace of life
that robs a person of serenity.

As we have considered how culture and things
intertwine, we have used speculations and have forced
data to illustrate the way the process might take place.
Neither the comparison of the Hoosier teenager with the
Guanacastecan, nor the comparisons among "Gladys,"
"Chepe," and "Ricardo" provide reliable data for
scientific use in testing any hypothesis about culture's
giving meaning to things. Another observer on another
occasion in another place might have carried out those
subjective exercises quite differently. I have merely tried
to illustrate, from personal experience in a culture
different from my own, the possibility that the peoples of
different cultures see things differently. The careful work
of the scientist should follow, testing hypotheses with
objective and verifiable data.

That data is available. Here is a sample. When Nelson

Rockefeller died in early 1979, he was remembered in the United States for his generosity and service. In Latin America he was remembered for one very bad gift. In the late 1960s he was sent by President Nixon on a goodwill mission to Latin America. In Honduras his visit caused anti-Yankee demonstrations which resulted in the death of a youth. Rockefeller, in sorrow, visited the youth's mother, and there met a younger brother of the victim. To show his love, Rockefeller offered the younger brother a scholarship to cover his future educational costs. That gift, which the North American culture interpreted as a symbol of remorse and recompense, fired up Latin Americans to new heights of hatred, for to them Rockefeller tried to buy off the blood of a martyr with dirty dollars.

All these things, be they *tamales* or *scholarships*, may not look the same from the other's point of view.

A Postscript

The careful reader may be asking, "Why should this book on cross-cultural communication end with a chapter about material *things*? Could there not be a more intellectual or spiritual finale?"

Surely enough, the chapter was about *tamales*, carpet and vacuum sweepers, a street cleaner, a box, and Nelson Rockefeller's gift-scholarship. I must admit that the chapter has a materialistic focus.

In defense of my decision to write about things, I would like to comment briefly on what I consider to be the most pervasive and influential incentive for world communication today. Let me begin by asking, *When two different cultures communicate with each other, what are the people talking about?* (In chapter two we discussed the "objects of communication" that make it possible for participant A and participant B to interact with each other.) The question seems innocent enough until one begins to examine and reject possible answers.

What do the people talk about? About religion? Well, missions have been important in the nineteenth and twentieth centuries, and there are relatively few countries of the world which have no foreign religious missions. It's a good answer, but not adequate, because missionaries and their communication with national peoples would represent too small a part of the whole of cross-cultural communication.

About education? That is, about curricula or textbooks or schools? No, there is relatively little communication across cultures on this crucial topic.

About the arts? To be sure, orchestras, ballet troupes, and opera companies tour the world, and poets and painters visit (or study) in other countries, but communication-about-art would represent a very small part of the international communication agenda.

What other possibilities are there? Athletics? Scientific tests? Natural disasters? Philosophical argumentation? But none of these is the principal incentive for cross-cultural interaction.

For a contemporary clue to the answer, consider the long decades in which the United States and the People's Republic of China did not communicate with each other. No embassies. No visas. The two countries were separated from each other by more than an ocean. Why? The obvious reason had to do with political antagonisms: the United States was supposedly free and democratic, China was supposedly communist. But then in an apparently strange exchange of gestures, communication

began. Strange, I say, because the political situation did
not change. The United States was still free and
democratic; China was still communist. Nonetheless the
gestures continued, even to the reestablishing of official
relationships. What prompted the new initiatives?
Religion? Education? The arts? Athletics? No, not these,
but rather Coca-Cola. It was the desire for the exchange of
consumer (and military) goods. *Things*.

In a similar case, when President Carter and President
Brezhnev met in Vienna in June 1979 to sign the Salt II
pact, the topic of their one private conversation was—you
guessed it, the U.S. restrictions on the importation of
Soviet goods. *Things*.

To the person traveling abroad, there is immediate
evidence of great enthusiasm—or hunger—for the
consumption of things. A wrist watch, jeans, John
Travolta records, color TV, Hollywood posters, T-shirts
with foreign insignia, cars, cassette players, and show-
cases of trivia.

When the peoples of two cultures communicate, the
chances are high that they are interacting over things. A
commerce of material objects. The manufacture, distribution, and consumption of products.

What is the consequence of "all these things?" In the
first place, I have tried to show in chapter seven that
because people see things from different points of view,
the objects themselves may take on cultural valuations. In
the end when two strangers try to talk with each other
about a particular object, their communication may fail
because the particular object is really two different
objects.

In the second place, I suggest that a world communication system whose messages are primarily commercial

could lead vast populations—particularly those with a hunger to enjoy material possessions—to live only to consume. In other words, the highest good in life would be nothing other than having as one's own the products huckstered in the marketplace, in the newspapers, and in the electronic media. A fear of the loss of deeper spiritual values prompted Julio Suñol, a journalist from Costa Rica, to write a biting caricature of the newly emerging consumer class:

> Don't be anxious about the middle class. Its people are conditioned by a society of consumption, not elevated by it. Do you really think this middle-class person would dare to give an opinion, to disagree, to confront us if he knew he might lose the automobile he's paying off in monthly installments, that he might lose the house he is paying off in meager monthly sums; if he suspects that he can no longer travel today and pay tomorrow; if he becomes aware that in expressing dissidence his own children can be expelled from the better schools? All these SOBs are the same: they pretend to be something they're not. And to live something one is not, one has to give up the little one is—the condition of being human. It's what these cowards have done, allowing themselves to be converted into big shots, into wise guys, yet mummies and sphinxes who don't read, nor study, and much less think. They have time only for watching television, taking a drink on weekends, fornicating, committing adultery, taking hardly a glance at the newspaper inasmuch as they can't read and they wouldn't want to waste time. . . .[4]

But there is yet another concern about the predominance of things in cross-cultural communication. The things are, in most cases products. Products move from one person to another. There may be payment of money or of products in exchange. It seems fair enough. But it isn't. To anyone who cares enough to find out, it is becoming more obvious each year that the exchange or sale of products on the international market is not benefiting everyone equally. The old cliché won't go away: the rich are getting richer, the poor poorer. On the one side are the individuals and companies (often multinational companies) who control the oil reserves of the earth, who have mastered the know-how of mechanical, electronic, and nuclear technology, and who guide the production and distribution of consumer goods. [5] On the other side are the disadvantaged, the laborers, the people who live from paycheck to paycheck—these are the peoples of earth who are attracted by the promotion of consumer goods and who hope that the goods will give them a better life. But the years and the decades reveal the disparities that will only increase the disillusionment of the peoples of the world.

If North Americans—and here I include myself and my readers—are going to improve the success of our cross-cultural communication, extending it over into educational and philosophical and spiritual areas, then we shall have to respond to the fact that we are on the side of the rich, on the side of the power brokers, on the side of the multinational companies, on the side of those who know how to use technology, on the side of the manufacturers and promotors, on the side of those who have just about everything they want.

That is, on the north side of the Rio Grande.

But being from the north side of the Rio Grande does not mean that we can't communicate with folks south of the River. It's easy to illustrate even from our own experience how a communication about and through *things* offers the potential for enriching all of us. In our most recent two-year stint in Costa Rica, we were given many lovely things: pineapples, a wooden bowl, mint, roses, a ceramic guitar, a piece of copper, a sea shell, a carved book holder, *plátanos*, *chiverre*, honeycomb, mangos, two orchid plants, *pan bon*, lettuce, *tamales* and of course coffee. And it was in Costa Rica where we learned to give flowers. Through gifts, and an exchange of things, friendships were formed and were cultivated.

And so cross-cultural communication about things is not, for us, a discouraging word.

Afterword

From Philippians 2

Let your bearing towards one another
   arise out of your life in Christ Jesus.
For the divine nature was his from the first;
yet he did not think to snatch at equality with God,
   but made himself nothing,
   assuming the nature of a slave.
   Bearing the human likeness,
   revealed in human shape,
   he humbled himself,
   and in obedience accepted even death —
      death on a cross.

Therefore God raised him to the heights
   and bestowed on him the name above all names,
that at the name of Jesus every knee should bow —
   in heaven, on earth, and in the depths —
   and every tongue confess,
"Jesus Christ is Lord."
to the glory of God the Father.

A paraphrase from Philippians 2

Let your cross-cultural perspectives have as their vantage point the life of Christ. For Christ belonged to a celestial culture, where he fit in perfectly enough to rank with the best.

But he put that aside and entered a terrestrial culture, carrying with him no extra baggage, no sense of superiority, no chauvinism, no presumptions. He joined its peoples, and became one of them until he not only could see from their point of view, but could live their kind of life.

His identification was so complete that he died for their cause. God noticed, and honored the venture by making Christ the universal focal point, in whom all people can have common vision.

Chart 1

Per Capita Income in Ten American Countries

Covering One Year from 1950, 51, 52, 53, 54, or 55, depending upon available information

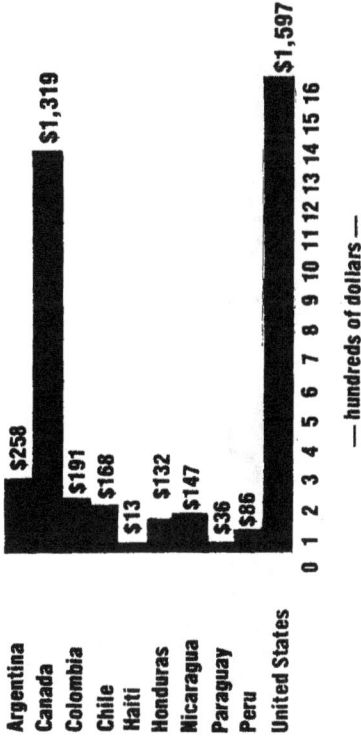

Country	Value
Argentina	$258
Canada	$1,319
Colombia	$191
Chile	$168
Haiti	$13
Honduras	$132
Nicaragua	$147
Paraguay	$36
Peru	$86
United States	$1,597

0 1 2 3 4 5 6 7 8 9 10 11 12 13 14 15 16

— hundreds of dollars —

source *Enciclopedia Barsa, Editores, Encyclopaedia Britannica, Buenos Aires, Chicago, Mexico, 1957.*

Chart 2

Per Capita Income in the Americas
Covering Year 1975 (exceptions +1973, ++1974, +++1976)

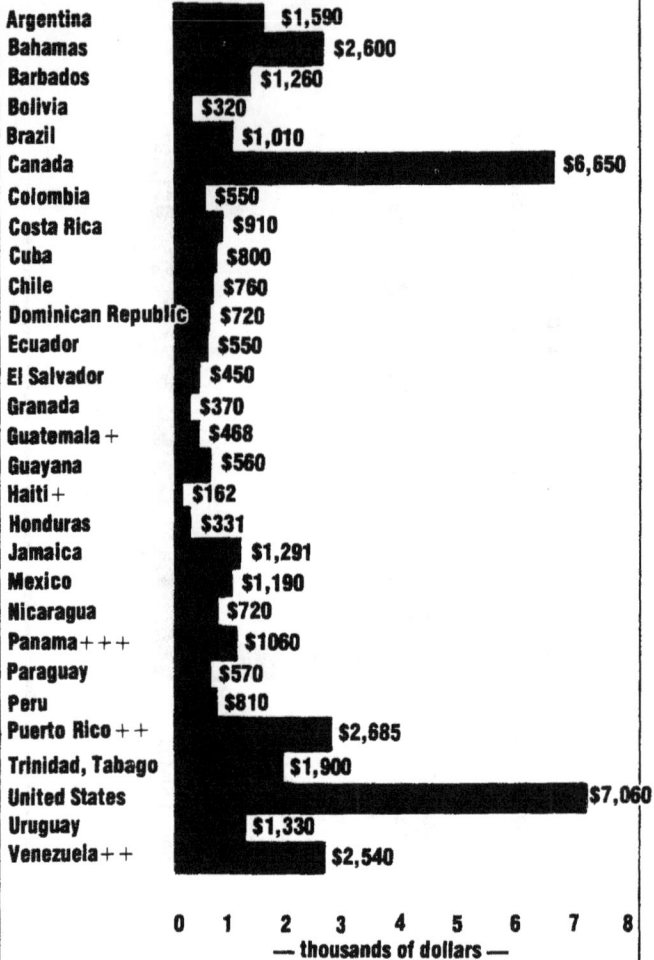

Argentina	$1,590
Bahamas	$2,600
Barbados	$1,260
Bolivia	$320
Brazil	$1,010
Canada	$6,650
Colombia	$550
Costa Rica	$910
Cuba	$800
Chile	$760
Dominican Republic	$720
Ecuador	$550
El Salvador	$450
Granada	$370
Guatemala +	$468
Guayana	$560
Haiti +	$162
Honduras	$331
Jamaica	$1,291
Mexico	$1,190
Nicaragua	$720
Panama+++	$1060
Paraguay	$570
Peru	$810
Puerto Rico ++	$2,685
Trinidad, Tabago	$1,900
United States	$7,060
Uruguay	$1,330
Venezuela++	$2,540

```
0   1   2   3   4   5   6   7   8
        — thousands of dollars —
```

source World Almanaque, 1978

End Notes

Introduction

1. Eugene A. Nida, *Understanding Latin Americans*, William Carey Library, 1974, p 3.

Chapter 1

1. Published by National Textbook Company, Skokie, Illinois, 1974.

2. Hall has delineated 10 primary message systems that all cultures use: interaction, association, subsistence, bisexuality, territoriality, temporality, learning, play, defense, and use of materials. *The Silent Language* is a Doubleday Anchor Book.

3. T. S. Eliot. "The Love Song of J. Alfred Prufrock."

4. For a copy of the brochure, write The Christophers, 12 East 48th Street, New York, N. Y. 10017.

Chapter 2

1. Cervantes, *Don Quixote*, trans Walter Starkie, Macmillan, 1957.

2. Richard P. Coleman and Lee Rainwater, *Social Standing in America: New Dimensions of Class*, Basic Books, 1978.

3. Written by Bella Stumbo, *The Miami Herald*, Sunday, October 1, 1978, p 4-BW.

4. Theodore M. Newcomb, "An Approach to the Study of Communicative Acts" in *Small Groups: Studies in Social Interaction*, edited by Hare, Borgatta, and Bales, Knopf, 1955.

5. L. John Martin, "The Contradiction of Cross-Cultural Communication," a paper read at the Seminar on Mass Communications, Mexico City, March 14, 1974, reprinted in *International and Intercultural*

Communication, edited by Heinz Dietrich Fischer and John C. Merrill, Hastings House, 1976, p 424.

6. Gerhard Maletzke, "Intercultural and International Communication" in Fischer and Merrill, p 409.

Chapter 3

1. Thomas P. McCann, *An American Company; The Tragedy of United Fruit*, edited by Henry Scammell, Crown Publishers, Inc., 1976, pp. 39-40.

2. Eleanor Johnson Tracy, "How United Brands Survived the Banana War," *Fortune*, July 19, 1976, p. 145 ff.

3. The figure is widely quoted. It is estimated that another 4,000 died before the entire railroad was finished. See *Keith y Costa Rica*, by Watt Stewart, translated by Jose B. Acuña, Editorial Costa Rica, 1976. Originally published under the title *Keith and Costa Rica*, University of New Mexico Press, 1964.

4. Howard I. Blutstein, et al, *Area Handbook for Costa Rica*, Foreign Area Studies, the American University, 1970, p. 21.

5. McCann, p. 15.

6. Stacy May and Galo Plaza, translated by Maria Cristina Cabezas, *La United Fruit Company en America Latina*, National Planning Association, 1958, p. 7.

7. May and Plaza, p. 6.

8. Stewart, p. 34

9. McCann, p. 16.

10. Donald E. Lundberg, *Costa Rica*, 3rd edition, 1976, p. 115 (published by Juan Mora F. Apdo 4160, San Jose, Costa Rica).

11. May and Plaza, p. 19.

12. McCann, p. 143.

13. McCann, p. 18.

14. May and Plaza, p. 8.

15. May and Plaza, p. 19.

16. McCann, p. 22.

17. McCann, p. 40.

18. May and Plaza, p. 116.

19. May and Plaza, pp. 123-125.

20. May and Plaza, p. 154.

21. "Sorting Out the Wreckage," *Fortune*, June 1975, p. 19.

22. John Kenneth Galbraith, "Bananas," a review of McCann's *An American Company*, in *The New York Review of Books*, October 14, 1976, p. 10 ff.

23. Galbraith, p. 10.

24. "Sorting Out the Wreckage," p. 19.

25. Tracy, p. 151.

26. Blutstein, et al, p. 210.

27. McCann, pp. 135-136.

28. Miguel Angel Asturias, *Strong Wind*, translated from the Spanish by Gregory Rabassa, A Laurel Edition by Dell Publishing Co., 1968. Originally published in Spanish under the title *Viento Fuerte* by Editorial Losada S.A. Buenos Aires, 1962.

29. Miguel Angel Asturias, *The Green Pope*, translated from the Spanish by Gregory Rabassa, Dell Publishing Co., 1971. Originally published in Spanish under the title El Papa Verde, Editorial Losada S.A. Bueno Aires, 1954.

30. Miguel Angel Asturias, *The Eyes of the Interred*, translated from the Spanish by Gregory Rabassa, by Dell Publishing Co., 1973. Originally published in Spanish under the title Los Ojos De Los Enterrados, Editorial Losada, S.A. Buenos Aires, 1960.

31. The book is billed as the "Seventh Case Study in a Series about United States Enterprises Abroad." It is published by the National Planning Association, with supporting funds from the Carnegie Corporation and the John Hay Whitney Foundation. While giving extensive facts about the company, the general tenor is clearly a defense of company policies.

32. Carlos Luis Fallas, *Mamita Yunai*, Published by Libreria Lehmann, San Jose. The first edition won the 1965-66 national literature award in Costa Rica.

33. Emir Rodriguez Monegal, *The Borzoi Anthology of Latin American Literature*, Volume II, Alfred A. Knopf, Inc., 1977. See "Miguel Angel Asturias," pp. 511-517.

34. McCann, pp. 151-153.

35. McCann, pp. 85 ff.

36. Galbraith, p. 10.

37. McCann, p. 21.

38. Galbraith, p. 10.

39. Tom Buckley, in a review of *An American Company* by McCann appearing in the *New York Times Book Review*, October 31, 1976, p. 7.

40. May and Plaza, p. 28.

41. Jose Miguez Bonino, *La fe en busca de eficacia*, Ediciones Sigueme, Salamanca, 1977, 37.

42. May and Plaza, p. 73.

43. Blutstein, et al, p. 189.

44. Denis Goulet, *The Cruel Choice; A New Concept in the Theory of Development*, Atheneum, New York, 1975, p. vii.

45. McCann, p. 34.

46. McCann, pp. 142-143.

47. Lundberg, p. 91.
48. May and Plaza, p. 81.
49. May and Plaza, p. 15.
50. Galbraith, p. 10.
51. McCann, p. 20.
52. Tracy, p. 146.
53. Presented to Goshen College students, Centro Cultural Costarricense-Norte Americano, July 10, 1978.
54. Buckley, p. 7.
55. May and Plaza, p. 26.
56. For more discussions of the Guatemala episode, see McCann, Chapter 4; May and Plaza, pp. 231-234; Pedro Urra Veloso, *La Guerra del Banano* (De la Mamita Yunai a la UPEB) Tierra Nueva, Argentina, 1975; and for a study of United Fruit's political program in Cuba see *United Fruit Company: Un Caso Del Dominio Imperialista en Cuba*, Editorial de Ciencias Sociales, La Habana, 1978.

Chapter 4

1. In 1968 in a conference of Latin American bishops in Medellin, Colombia, the historically conservative hierarchy "renounced its ties with the continent's military, landowning, and industrial interests in the cause of social justice . . . the cost of this commitment has been extraordinary. Church sources estimate that some 850 bishops, priests, and nuns have been arrested, tortured, exiled, or killed in the past decade. Thousands of laymen have similarly suffered in the military regimes governing two thirds of the Latin American people." Penny Lernoux, "Latin's Church Is Facing a Crossroads," *The Miami Herald*, Thursday, November 16, 1978, p. 3-AW.
2. "My point of departure should be kept clearly in mind," said J. L. Segundo. "It is the following: America Latina." J. A. Hernandez, *Esbozo para una teologia de la liberacion*. (Ed. Prosencia, Bogota, 1970) II p. 37.
3. "Magazine Publisher Slain in Argentine" *The Miami Herald*, August 30, 1978, p. 3-AW.
4. "Bolivia" *Almanaque Mundial 1978*, Panama: Editorial America, S.A. pp. 138-142.
5. "Brazil's Wasted Generation," *Time*, September 11, 1978, pp. 11-12.
6. Penny Lernoux, "Shaky Democracy Confronts Turbay in Colombia Rule," *The Miami Herald*, August 6, 1978, p. 3-AW.
7. See again Chapter 3. To the credit of the fruit company, it has entered into negotiations with Costa Rica's president, Rodrigo Carazo, to reduce the tenure of the current contract law by 10 years. The law

was signed in 1938, and was to run until 1988!

8. See *Cristo Vivo en Cuba* (Departmento Ecumenico de Investigaciones, San Jose, Costa Rica) particularly the Appendix which includes a transcript of a meeting of President Castro with members of the church of Jamaica, held October 20, 1977.

9. Charles Padilla "Five Years After Allende, Chile's Junta Keeps Firm Grip on Country," *The Miami Herald*, Tuesday, September 12, 1978, p. 3.

10. In 1915 the United States demanded the nomination of a North American economic council and the creation of a police corps under the command of a marine official. When confusions and fighting resulted, the U.S. sent a contingent of marines and by November 29, 1916 established a military regiment that endured until 1924. Again in 1965, after several years of internal political chaos, the U.S. intervened with marine infantry until the Organization of American States assumed control.

11. "Ecuador," *Almanaque Mundial* 1978, pp. 172-176.

12. See *Coffee, The Rules of the Game, and You*, by Thomas Fenton, published by the Christophers, 12 East 48th Street, New York, NY 10017.

13. "Guatemala," *Almanaque Mundial* 1978, pp. 192-196.

14. Those figures were mentioned by Guatemalan seminarians in a convocation program, Latin American Biblical Seminary, September 14, 1978. The booklet *Situación Politica en Guatemala* (Coleccion Cuadernos Cedal, Costa Rica, 1974) closes with these words: "En tanto persista el actual régimen económico y las secuelas de explotación y de dependencia externa, por encima de los textos legales existentes o por existir, el régimen democrático se hace imposible, puesto que el instrumento básicamente utilizado por la oligarquía sigue siendo la violencia en todas sus variantes, desde el despotismo, la miseria, la desnutricion y la explotación económica, hasta la tortura, el asesinato y el genocidio, en fin, el terror en todas sus formas."

15. Karen DeYoung, " 'Baby Doc' Has Grown But Haiti's About Same," *The Miami Herald*, Friday, September 15, 1978, p. 3-AW.

16. "U.S. to Double Aid to Haiti If Wide Reforms Are Made," *The Miami Herald*, August 25, 1978, p. 3-AW.

17. *Almanaque Mundial* 1978, "Honduras," pp. 202-206.

18. "80 Mexican Women Start Hunger Strike," *The Miami Herald*, August 30, 1978, p. 3-AW.

19. "Mexican President in Dilemma Over Terms of Amnesty Proposal," *The Miami Herald*, Sept. 14, 1978, p. 3-AW.

20. The first Somoza, Anastasio, was brought to power in 1933 through U.S. assistance. (U.S. military forces occupied the country

from 1922 to 1925 and 1926 to 1933.) President Anastasio Somoza was assassinated in 1956 and was succeeded by his son Luis. Anastasio, Jr., assumed the presidency in 1967. There have been interim presidents, but always handpicked by the Somozas. Anastasio, Jr., was trained at West Point. See Richard Millett, *Guardians of the Dynasty: A History of the Somoza Dynasty and the U.S.-Created Guardia Nacional de Nicaragua.*

21. The Senator from California, after long personal turmoils, voted for treaty ratification, and later said that his statement was meant as a joke.

22. "Un dolor de cabeza para Stroessner," *Visión*, Vol 51, No. 5, August 25, 1978, p. 16.

23. Georgie Anne Geyer, *The New Latins: Fateful Change in South and Central America*, Doubleday, 1970, p. 1973. See all of chapter 9 on the Inca Renaissance in the Andes. The miners' strike took place during July and August of 1978.

24. A former resident of Uruguay, whose identity is being withheld, claims that up to 40 percent of the population has fled the country due to economic privation and cruel repression by the government. The government, of course, denies the exodus. The source adds, "Our friends, who ten years ago were affluent enough to spend vacations in Argentina, today question how they will put food on the table."

25. The rapid increase in the price of oil quickly brought millions of dollars to the already wealthy Venezuelan elite. How to spend the money has been a problem for them; no matter how much they spend, there is still lots left over. Fidel Castro charged that the Organization of Petroleum Exporting Nations (OPEC), of which Venezuela is a member, are "reactionary sultans" who are "being fed with the sweat and hunger of hundreds of millions in the Third World." J. P. Smith, "Opec's Wealth Causes Rift with Rest of Third World," *The Miami Herald*, Wednesday, September 20, 1978, p. 3-AW.

26. Matthew 26:11; Mark 14:7; John 12:8.

27. Jose Miguez Bonino, *La fe en busca de eficacia; Una interpretacion de la reflexion teologica latinoamericana de liberacion.* (Ediciones Sigueme, Salamanca, 1977). He deals in chapter 2 with the disillusionment resulting from the decades of development.

28. To put the phrase into a concrete context: Costa Ricans were told in the 1960s by economic advisers from the United States to diversify their national product—to raise cattle, for example. Ranchers in Guanacaste and San Carlos and Perez Zeledon complied by investing deeply in cattle. When Costa Rica's meat was ready for the international market, U.S. meat raisers lobbied Congress for quotas and higher tariffs that would keep foreign meat out of the country, and

thus their own meat could be sold at a higher price. Costa Rica's ranchers were the obvious losers.

29. After reams of denials by CIA spokesmen, we have gradually learned months or even years later of the many CIA initiatives in Latin American politics, the most recent being its attempts to oust Castro and its role in Allende's overthrow. We are told that "national security" justifies such interventions. To Latin Americans, however, the CIA means an international Gestapo.

30. Miguez Bonino, p. 37.

31. Among the most perceptive studies of the Latin American personality is Eugene Nida's *Understanding Latin Americans* (William Carey Library, South Pasadena, California, 1974). He discusses the value systems and personality traits in terms of three major sets of contrasting features: (1) authoritarianism vs. individualism, (2) idealism vs. realism, and (3) *machismo* vs. *hembrismo*.

32. See Jose Miguez Bonino, "Nuevas Perspectivas Teologicas" (A paper presented at the Fifth Institute and General Assembly of the World Council of Christian Education, Huampani, Peru, July 12-21, 1971).

33. See Hugo Assmann, *Teologia desde la praxis de la liberacion: Ensayo teologico desde la America decendiente,* 2nd edition. (Ediciones Sigueme, Salamance, 1976). The book has been translated into English as *Theology for a Nomad Church* (New York: Orbis Books, 1976).

34. Miguez Bonino ("Nuevas Perspectivas Teologicas"), in describing the current situation, already hints strongly at the kinds of tools needed to understand and solve the problems:

(1) We perceive our historical reality has been determined by conflict and not by evolution.

(2) The only significant analysis of that reality must consider structural components.

(3) The instruments for the analysis must come from the political and social sciences.

(4) The analysis proceeds toward a taking of an ideological position.

(5) There aren't neutral sciences of society and man.

(6) Study and thought must lead to action, to a struggle to transform our historical reality.

35. See Raul Vidales, "Cuestiones en torno al método en la teología de la liberación," Servicio de Documentación MIEC-JECI (Lima, 1974).

36. In spite of the fact that the Latin American church hierarchy has remained very largely antisocialistic, and in spite of the warning of Pope John Paul I — in his first public political statement (Wednesday,

September 20, 1978) — that Catholics should not look for their salvation in the maxims of Lenin, and the rejection by Pope John Paul II of socialism, the young theologians and sociologists and opinion leaders of Latin America identify with Marxism. See, for example, Victorio Araya, *Fe Cristiana y Marxismo: Una Perspectiva Latinoamericana* (San Jose, Litografia Lehmann, 1974).

37. Karl Marx's most widely known writings are *The Communist Manifesto*, written in collaboration with his good friend Friedrich Engels in 1848, and *Das Kapital*, whose first volume was published in 1867. Both are available in Penquin paperbacks.

38. Mariano Grondona, "La agonia del capitalismo," Informe Especial en *Visión*, August 11, 1978, pp. 6-15.

39. An interesting summary of liberal, Western thought, written from a Latin American point of view is provided by Gustavo Gutierrez, *Teología desde el reverso de la historia*, Centro de Estudios y Publicaciones, Jiron Puno 387 - Of. 506, Apartado 6118. T. 281858, Lima Peru, February 1977. John Knox Press has released the book in English — *Liberation and Change* (1977).

40. Gustavo Gutierrez, Teologia desde el reverso de la historia.

41. See the two volumes entitled *Capitalismo: Violencia y Anti-Vida: La opresión de las mayorías y la domesticación de los dioses*, edited by Elsa Tamez y Saul Trinidad (papers contributed to the Latin American Encounter of Social Scientists and Theologians sponsored by the Conferación Superior Universitaria Centroamericana, February 21-25, 1978, in San Jose, Costa Rica, and published by Editorial Universitaria Centro Americana, 1978).

42. Araya, p. 151.

43. Gutierrez, *Teologia desde el reverso de la historia*, p. 44.

44. In chapter 4 of *La Fe en busca de eficacia*, Miguez Bonino discusses the theological reflections of four people: Juan Luis Segundo, Uruguayan Jesuit; Lucio Gera, Argentine priest, Gustavo Gutierrez, Peruvian priest; and Hugo Assman, Brazilian sociologist. The following listing was suggested by an intermixing of the thought of these four leaders.

45. See Exodus 1—18. In "Revelación y Anuncio de Dios en la Historia," Gustavo Guttierez traces the major strands of liberation thought in the Scriptures.

46. Principally Isaiah, Jeremiah, Hosea, Joel, Amos, and Micah.

47. Luke 4:18, 19.

48. Jesus said:

How blest are you who are in need; the kingdom of God is yours.
How blest are you who now go hungry; your hunger shall be satisfied.
How blest are you who weep now; you shall laugh. . . .

Alas for you who are rich; you have had your time of happiness.
Alas for you who are well-fed now; you shall go hungry.
Alas for you who laugh now; you shall mourn and weep.
Luke 6:20, 21, 24, 25.

49. Elsa Tamez provides a helpful reading of the Scriptures in *La Hora de la Vida*. Departamento Ecumenico de Investigaciones, Apartado 339, San Pedro Montes de Oca, San Jose, Costa Rica, 1978. She contrasts the passages about death and life, rich and poor, oppressor and oppressed.

50. Tamez, pp. 96, 97.

51. Miguez Bonino, quoting Pedro Aran in a theological colloquium on "The Authority of the Bible" at the meeting of the Latin American Evangelical Theology Association, Cochabamba, Bolivia, December 1971.

52. "Hermenéutica, verdad y praxis" is a full-chapter reply concerning the ideologization of Scriptures in Miguez Bonino *La fe en busca de eficacia*.

53. Orlando E. Costas, "Liberation Theology: A Solution?" *The Mennonite*, July 11, 1978, pp. 433-435.

54. One recent study has been John Howard Yoder's *The Politics of Jesus* (Eerdmans, 1972). Yoder is quoted in a profile in *Festival Quarterly* (February-March-April 1978, p. 15) as saying the book "found an audience at the right time. The evangelicals were looking for something social and the ecumenists were looking for something more biblical."

55. Gutierrez, "El evangelio y praxis de liberación," in *Fe cristiana y cambio social en America Latina*, Salamanca, Ediciones Sigueme, 1973, p. 234.

56. Miguez Bonino, *La Fe en busca de eficacia*, p. 112.

57. Again, Rosa Maria is referring to Miguez Bonino's writings, as found in *La Fe en busca de eficacia*, chapter 6 entitled "Amor, reconciliacion y conflicto." See also "Critica al concepto corriente de violencia" which is chapter 8 of Hugo Assmann's *Teologia desde la Praxis de la Liberación*.

58. Matthew 26:52.

59. John 18:36.

60. "John Paul vs Liberation Theology" *Time*, February 12, 1979, pp. 28 and 29. See also the 8,000-word final statement debated and finally approved by the bishops which, according to *Time*, February 26, 1979, p. 50, contained a stronger mandate for church involvement in social issues than had been expected. The papal encyclical, "The Redemption of Man," was released in March of 1979, less than a month after the visit to Mexico.

Chapter 5
1. "U.S. Hispanics; An Awakening Minority," a cover story in *Time*, October 16, 1978, pp. 12-19.
2. Leonel J. Castillo, "Como controlar la inmigración," *Visión*, May 19, 1978, pp. 14, 15.
3. Penny Lernoux, "Latins' Church Is Facing a Crossroads," *The Miami Herald*, November 16, 1978.
4. William Chilett, London Observer Service. "U.S. Steps to Curb Wetbacks Stir Fury on Other Side of the 'Tortilla Curtain,'" *The Miami Herald*, November 18, 1978, p. 3-AW.
5. The Herald Latin American Staff, "Latin Population Continues Climb," *The Miami Herald*, Monday, October 2, 1978, p. 3-AW.
6. "Los indocumentados," a special report in *Visión*, May 19, 1978, pp. 6-15.
7. William R. Long, "Mexico and Its Expected Oil Reserves," *The Miami Herald*, November 19, 1978, p. 3-AW.

Chapter 7
1. Edward Hall, *The Silent Language* (Anchor Press/Doubleday, 1973), p. 57.
2. From Galen's unpublished journal. Used with permission.
3. Denis Goulet, *The Cruel Choice* (Atheneum, New York, 1975) pp. 23, 24.
4. Julio Suñol, *La Noche de los Tiburones* (Imprenta Lehmann, 1977) p. 49. Translated by the author.
5. Herbert I. Schiller, in *Communication and Cultural Domination* (International Arts and Sciences Press, Inc. 1976) pp. 49 and 50 writes: Technology, which appears mainly, and is almost exclusively understood, as visible machinery and hardware, lends itself admirably to the claim that it is neutral, value free, and employable under *any* social order, for sometimes quite different ends. . . . (But it is in reality) a one-way street for exercising domination by the already-powerful . . . with the still greater likelihood of intensifying the dependency of the weaker parties.

For Further Reading and Study

Cherry, Colin. *World Communication: Threat or Promise.* John Wiley and Sons, 1971.

"Communication and Integrated Development," *ICIT* Report No 16, October 1976. (Information Center on Instructional Technology, 1414 22nd St., N.W. Washington, D.C. 20037.)

Fersh, Seymour, ed. *Learning about People and Cultures.* McDougal, Little and Co., 1974.

Fischer, Heinz-Dietrich and John C. Merrill. *International and Intercultural Communication.* Hastings House, 1976.

Fuglesand, Andreas. *Doing Things . . . Together.* Uppsala, Sweden: Dag Hammarskjold Foundation (address: Ovre Slottsgata 2, S-752, 20, Uppsala), 1977.

Gorden, Raymond L. *Living in Latin America.* National Textbook Co., 1974.

Goulet, Denis. *The Cruel Choice: A New Concept in the Theory of Development.* Atheneum, 1975.

Hall, Edward T. *The Silent Language.* Doubleday, 1959.

Herskovits, Melville J. *Cultural Relativism.* Random House, 1972.

Hess, J. Daniel. *Integrity: Let Your Yea be Yea.* Herald Press, 1978.

Hogard, Richard. *On Culture and Communication.* Oxford University Press, 1972.

Nida, Eugene A. *Understanding Latin Americans: With Special*

Reference to Religious Values and Movements. William Carey Library, 1974.

Oberg, Dalervo. "Culture Shock and the Problems of Adjustment to New Cultural Environments" in *Ideas, Customs and Peoples.* International Voluntary Service.

Prosser, Michael H., ed. *Intercommunication Among Nations and Peoples.* Harper and Row, 1973.

Samover, L. A. and Richard Porter, eds. *Intercultural Communication: A Reader.* Wadsworth Publishing Co. 1972.

Shenk, Wilbert R. "The Stuff of Which Missionaries Are Made," *Gospel Herald*, May 23, 1978, p. 406.

Sider, Roger C. "The Missionary as a Marginal Person," *Mission Focus.* Vol. VI, Number 3, January 78.

Swartzendruber, Jan. "An Ethic for Communication in International Development," unpublished paper, Senior Communication Seminar, Goshen College, April 1977.

The author grew up on a farm near Lancaster, Pennsylvania. *("Not until I entered the town's consolidated school did I realize that I was a country boy.")*

He is a graduate of Eastern Mennonite College, Harrisonburg, Virginia. *("Not until I went to Virginia did I realize that I was a Pennsylvania Dutchman.")*

For two years he worked in the Voluntary Service program of the Mennonite Board of Missions, Elkhart, Indiana. *("Not until I lived in Indiana did I realize that I was an Easterner.")*

He earned masters and doctors degrees from Syracuse University, Syracuse, New York. *("Not until I enrolled in graduate school did I realize that I was a Mennonite.")*

Since 1964 he has been on the staff of Goshen College, Goshen, Indiana, where he is professor of communication and for four years (1968, 1969, 1978, 1979) he directed the college's international program in Costa Rica. *("Not until I left the United States did I realize that I was a citizen of the United*

States, and depending where I was, a yankee, a gringo, an Anglo-Saxon, a capitalist, an imperialist, or a rich man.")

Hess has written for *Journalism Quarterly, Christian Living, Gospel Herald, The Writer, With,* and *Mennonite Weekly Review.* He is author of *Integrity: Let Your Yea Be Yea* (Herald Press, 1978); *Ethics in Business and Labor* (Herald Press, 1977); *Vignettes of Spain* (Pinchpenny Press, 1975); and *Writing to a Reader* (Goshen College, 1967).

Dan and Joy (Glick) Hess are the parents of Courtney Pierre, Gretchen Maria, Ingrid Susan, and Laura Elizabeth. They are members of College Mennonite Church, Goshen, Indiana.